Creating Caring
and Capable Boards

Creating Caring and Capable Boards

Reclaiming the Passion for Active Trusteeship

Katherine Tyler Scott

Jossey-Bass Publishers • San Francisco

> Jossey-Bass books and products are available through most bookstores. To contact Jossey-Bass directly, call (888) 378–2537, fax to (800) 605–2665, or visit our website at www.josseybass.com.
>
> Substantial discounts on bulk quantities of Jossey-Bass books are available to corporations, professional associations, and other organizations. For details and discount information, contact the special sales department at Jossey-Bass.

 Manufactured in the United States of America on Lyons Falls Turin Book. This paper is acid-free and 100 percent totally chlorine-free.

Library of Congress Cataloging-in-Publication Data

Tyler Scott, Katherine, 1943–
 Creating caring and capable boards: reclaiming the passion for active trusteeship / Katherine Tyler Scott.—1st ed.
  p. cm.—(The Jossey-Bass nonprofit and public management series)
Includes bibliographical references and index.
 ISBN 0-7879-4293-6 (hard: alk. paper)
 1. Nonprofit organizations—Management. 2. Leadership. 3. Trusts and trustees.
I. Title: Reclaiming the passion for active trusteeship. II. Title. III. Series.
 HD62.6.T93 2000
 658.4'22—dc21

                     99-050817

FIRST EDITION
HB Printing 10 9 8 7 6 5 4 3 2 1

The Jossey-Bass
Nonprofit and Public Management Series

To Fred,
who has held me in trust
and whose life exemplifies trusteeship

Contents

Preface

In 1986 while directing the Lilly Endowment Leadership Education Program (LELEP), a statewide leadership education program for youth-serving professionals in Indiana, several Lilly Fellows and I developed and field-tested an educational resource for boards of youth-serving organizations. Our work was prompted by two questions:

- How can the governance of institutions in the not-for-profit sector be improved?
- How can we prepare effective leadership for organizations?

Our work was influenced by the following factors:

- The knowledge that a vision of transforming Indiana into a state that genuinely cares for youth could not be achieved without also educating the boards of youth-serving agencies
- The need to develop resources for trustees that were compatible in quality and content with those produced by the Center for Early Adolescence for program staff, which we used with the fifty-two Lilly Fellows
- The experience of participating in an assemblage of researchers, practitioners, and scholars convened by the Lilly Endowment to engage in a depth exploration of and conversation about trusteeship and leadership

The convergence of these three elements set me on a journey of ongoing asking and learning about leadership in general and not-for-profit governance leadership in particular.

From the beginnings of my work with program and governance leaders and colleagues, I recognized the unique and powerful role that trustees have in the formation, development, and survival of not-for-profit organizations. This level of organizational leadership requires preparation that goes beyond the usual education for administrative and fiduciary responsibilities to one that develops a deeper understanding of the leadership responsibilities of boards.

The origins of Trustee Leadership Development's work reflect these beliefs and have helped to shape our educational pedagogy and products. We have developed a variety of resources for not-for-profit boards and have expanded our work to increase leadership grounded in the capacity to hold in trust in other sectors and in the community at large.

This book is about trustee leadership and the education and preparation needed to help boards exercise effective governance. Trustees of course need preparation for fiscal prudence; administrative, organizational, and procedural responsibilities; or specific skills and competencies in such areas as fundraising or marketing. They also need *depth education,* which helps them attain a deeper level of understanding of the character and culture of an organization. Depth education takes the leader beyond the surface to the deeper levels of institutional life, from which spring the organization's beliefs, attitudes, assumptions, and behavior. It involves learning about organizational history and mission, and understanding context and vision. Depth education brings to the exercise of trustee responsibilities a coherent and overarching framework within which the myriad tasks of running an organization can be effectively understood and exercised. Depth education is intended to strengthen trustees' ability to act with both knowledge and wisdom, to care with competence, to "hold the organization in trust."™ This key concept was missing from most educational approaches and offerings to boards and other leadership groups. Depth education stresses the importance of helping not-for-profit boards stretch the definition of their role to include that of being trustees with significant leadership responsibilities.

Altering the traditional practices of trustee and leadership education will require a strategic and wide-reaching effort. A number of individuals and organizations are interested in these issues, and many are contributing to a growing movement to improve the state of governance and leadership in the not-for-profit sector. This is a propitious time to galvanize such efforts, initiate deeper conversation and collaboration, and re-create a sector that is so central to our formation as human beings, institutions, and communities.

We are in an enormously important historical period, a time of defining transition. We need a fundamental change in the way we perceive and develop leadership—one that will appreciably change the future for the better. To ensure such a change means fostering a different kind of thinking in those who assume or will assume responsibilities for trusteeship and leadership of our institutions.

It is frequently said that volunteers give of their time, talent, and treasure. *Creating Caring and Capable Boards: Reclaiming the Passion for Active Trusteeship* adds a fourth "T" word to the conversation that leaders who govern bring to the not-for-profit sector: trust.

The capacity to participate and lead responsibly, whether in an organization or in community, is not innate; it is consciously and intentionally developed. An understanding of the vital connections between voluntarism and the corporate health of the citizenry is integral to effective trustee leadership. I believe it can be taught and learned in new and deeper ways that ultimately benefit us all.

Much voluntary activity and leadership is exercised through board service, and this book focuses on this activity. It is an invitation to those who care about and work in and with not-for-profit organizations to examine the quality of leadership exercised on boards. The information and process explored here can enable leaders to enter reverently and deeply, respectfully and capably into the deeper levels of organizational life, to mine what is precious and core to its identity and purpose, to determine with whom and how its gifts can be shared, and to nurture its future growth.

This book was written especially for not-for-profit executive, program, and governance leaders and board education and leadership development consultants and practitioners. It can be used as a resource for grounding a staff and board in a philosophy of service and a process of leadership education that can provide a framework for carrying out their responsibilities more effectively. The transformation and survival of not-for-profit organizations and the ability to deliver vital services to millions of Americans rests in the hands of these leaders. We must equip them to assume their responsibilities with competence, compassion, skill, and empathy.

Such examination will lead to renewed commitment to and improvement of the not-for-profit sector through intentional, reflective education that moves volunteers beyond basic management and administrative skills to a level of trusteeship where the capacity to lead can also be developed. This book describes the process and practices for attaining this level of governance leadership.

Chapter One traces the rich historical roots of voluntary service from which we have inherited a legacy of trusteeship, and identifies the possibility that we are losing a tradition of service, which prompts the need for a different education for trusteeship.

Chapter Two discusses some of the societal and cultural forces contributing to the demise of a language and practice of caring that endangers the legacy of trusteeship.

Chapter Three introduces the cornerstone concept for developing the capacity of leaders who can hold organizations in trust. What it means to hold something in trust is explored in depth, beginning with the origins of developing this capacity.

Chapter Four moves into a more reflective personal place of discernment about the nature of trusteeship and the ways in which it combines being and doing. The schism between being and doing reveals some of the reasons for the need to be more intentional about the ways in which we educate boards.

Chapter Five offers a framework for understanding trusteeship as a convergence of altruism and authority. The model can be a useful tool for assessing voluntary leadership and determining appropriate educational intervention and development.

Chapter Six explores the formation and discipline of giving and its deep spiritual roots and connection to the practices of trusteeship.

Chapters Seven and Eight introduce the process cycle for depth education and offer ways to determine organizational readiness for experiencing this approach.

Chapters Nine through Thirteen move into the organizational assessment phase and the other core elements in depth education: history, mission, publics, and future. Resources that may be useful in understanding and applying these concepts can be found at the end of the book.

Chapter Fourteen describes the split between the being and doing of leadership and its potentially negative impact on the practice of trusteeship. A particular view of leadership has an effect on a board's behavior and its capacity to engage in adaptive work that serves a larger good.

In communities across the country, Americans come together with shared concerns and hopes, tethered to a tradition and legacy of service. In the face of vast and multifaceted issues—education, employment, children and youth, race relations, economic development, poverty, environment, and others—we sustain the belief that we can change these conditions for the better.

Our hopes rest with the millions of volunteers who care about and are committed to helping others—with those who trust that their actions can improve the lives of others. It is a trust rooted in our history and one that will grow in the future if we nurture it. The challenge before us is how to enliven and implement our beliefs and hopes. Meeting this challenge is the mark of our character as a people, of our identity as a nation, of our future as a democracy.

Indianapolis, Indiana   KATHERINE TYLER SCOTT
December 1999

Acknowledgments

Writing has always been a labor of love for me. Something of this scope could not be done without both the labor and love of many individuals. I am grateful to Lilly Endowment, Inc., for its funding of Trustee Leadership Development, Inc. (TLD) and especially for the shared passion and commitment to the not-for-profit sector that Susan Wisely and Craig Dykstra represent. Special thanks and gratitude go to Susan for her wise counsel over the years.

I am appreciative of the trustee educators and program associates who are committed to work with executive and governance leaders; of the hundreds of not-for-profits and thousands of trustees whose many gifts contribute daily to the betterment of society; of the contributions of Parker Palmer to a deepened understanding of what it means to hold something in trust; and of the staff of TLD (particularly Lynn Flanagan for her able administrative assistance in the creation of this book), whose competence and professionalism have helped to create a special resource for not-for-profit leaders.

Many times I have marveled at the patience of my original editor, Alan Shrader, and his unwavering hope that something that might be useful to others would result from my efforts. The support of Dorothy Hearst and the assistance of Carolyn Uno are also deeply appreciated.

I am especially grateful to Fred and Frederick for their continual support, patience, and encouragement.

K.T.S.

The Author

Katherine Tyler Scott is the executive director of Trustee Leadership Development, a national leadership education program whose purpose is to improve the capacity of organizations to serve more responsibly and to lead more effectively. Before directing the Trustee Leadership Development program, she developed and directed the Lilly Endowment Leadership Education Program.

Tyler Scott has developed leadership training programs and resources for the National Association for Community Leadership and the National Episcopal Church. She helped develop the Episcopal Church "Women of Vision" training and the *GATES* Training materials for Phase II of the Episcopal Church Women Leadership Program. She is coauthor of several publications, including *Stories from the Circle: Women's Leadership in Community* (1991) and *The Inner Work of the Leader: Discovering the Leader Within* (1998). She is a contributing author to the book *Spirit at Work,* edited by Jay Conger (1994). She also chaired and helped develop *Finding Common Ground,* a training curriculum for community-wide dissemination administered through the Indiana University POLIS Center and the Indianapolis Urban League.

Tyler Scott is the recipient of the Sagamore of the Wabash, the highest honor the governor of Indiana can bestow on a citizen, and was awarded the first Indiana Youth Institute's Pathfinder Award in 1989 for her work in leadership education. She was the 1990 recipient of the Edna B. Lacy Service Award for her contribution and service to the Indianapolis community. In addition, she received the Distinguished Leadership Award from the National Association for Community Leadership in recognition of exemplary community service.

Her vocation is the preparation, development, and nurturance of leadership that holds individuals, organization, and communities in trust.

Part One

Understanding Trusteeship

Chapter One

Recovering a Tradition of Trusteeship

There are more than 1 million not-for-profit organizations in the United States, and each year 100,000 more are created. They comprise a sector that spends more than $1 trillion annually, ranking eighth among the world economies and employing more civilians than the federal and fifty state governments. Its boundaries encircle a variety of institutions and associations: libraries, social service agencies, hospitals, schools, churches, museums, colleges, universities, charities, and foundations. One of the unique features of this sector is its dependence on volunteers to help provide direct services, programs, and financial support and to ensure its very existence (Hodgkinson and others, 1992, p. 46). Ninety-three million Americans, or 48.8 percent, volunteer an average of 4.2 hours a week, representing a value of $201.5 billion annually (INDEPENDENT SECTOR, 1996).

Not only are Americans generous with their time; they also are generous with their money: 90 percent of all giving to nonprofits comes from individuals: "Nine out of ten adults are regular givers, and half of all living gifts come from families with incomes under $20,000" (Hodgkinson and others, 1992, p. 46). In 1996, Americans donated $122.22 billion to these organizations. "By any measure—size, economic impact, political influence, cultural role, effect on personal and social values, effect on public policy, or international presence—private nonprofit organizations hold a highly important position in American life" (O'Neill, 1989, p. 169).

This sector is one in which a diverse population can come together in substantive, sustained conversations about significant community issues and needs, formulate effective programmatic responses, and help shape public debate and policy. The state of this sector not only reflects our national character; it provides the opportunities and experiences that form and give it shape. The importance of developing and improving leadership in this sector cannot be overestimated; it is the nexus in which the country's economic, philanthropic, service, and religious interests intersect. Those who serve as leaders in and for this sector are the carriers of the culture's social conscience and have a major influence on the quality and well-being of our lives and our communities. Much of the service to others occurs through not-for-profit organizations; therefore, we must make every effort to ensure that those who serve and lead them are well equipped to carry out the good intended.

Cradled deep within the statistics are numerous stories, remarkable gifts of service, and a continuous sharing of time, talent, and money—gifts given to others, many of whom are not, and never will be, known by the donors. Millions of Americans donate billions of hours and dollars annually to numerous causes that address the needs of individuals they do not personally know. Why? Why do we give to the stranger? Why do we care about the needs of others who reside outside our private circle? What provokes us to set aside individual interests and concerns and attend to the broader interests and concerns of community? Why do we want to make a difference in the conditions of others' lives? The answers to these questions are not simple or easy, and those that do come to mind immediately are not etched in concrete. The answers we seek will be revealed over time and through experience. Some of them are embedded in the history of voluntary leadership in the not-for-profit sector. Our understanding of this story reveals a valuable American legacy of service and leadership unique to our culture and essential not only to the survival of the nonprofit sector but to the retention of democracy.

From the Pilgrims' social compact in 1620 to more contemporary national and local service initiatives, leaders have invited American citizens to live out a covenant "to care for each other's good and the whole by everyone and so mutually" (Ellis and Noyes, 1990, p. 18). The words that John Winthrop delivered in a sermon in 1630 in Salem Harbor provide an eloquent and archetypal refrain: "We must delight in each other, make others' conditions our own, rejoice together, mourn together, labor and suffer together, always having before our eyes our community as members of the same body" (Winthrop, 1965, p. 93). Similar covenantal beliefs and practices existed in other ethnic and religious groups. Many of the stories of Native Americans, African slaves, and other immigrants convey a strong ethic of altruism even during sustained periods of social, political, and economic marginalization. These philanthropic practices run deep within the American psyche and are intricately woven into our culture.

Voluntary action on behalf of the common good is the inherited legacy of every American, and gives life to an abiding belief that we share responsibility for the creation and quality of community life. We are identifiers of issues, needs, and problems, and we frequently expect to participate in the decision making about how to respond to them. Virtually every significant social movement in U.S. history originated in the voluntary sector: care for the mentally ill, civil rights, environmental stewardship, public education, health care, family planning, social welfare, political reform, and women's rights, among others. As John D. Rockefeller (1983, p. 369) observed, "These multitudinous social action movements of the third sector are not only bulwarks and defenses, they are also active creative forces for the continuous adaptation of our society to new needs and priorities and for its continuous revitalization. They are the seedbeds from which most important reforms in our country have begun. . . . Without the opportunity for such manifestations of citizen initiative . . . the American system would progressively lose its resilience and ultimately destroy its own legitimacy."

The third sector is an arena in which American citizens, individually and collectively, can give expression to the values of caring and compassion for others, who though they may be strangers are still felt to be a part of the community to which we all belong. It is in such expression that the capacity is fostered to create healthier organizations and public life. Within this vast network of service organizations, connections are made between individual interests and those of the whole community, and the tensions that exist between them and are continually encountered are transformed. The encounter with and transformation of these tensions transports us to a greater sense of relatedness and belonging—into an experience of dialogue about things that ultimately define individual identity and national character and that provide opportunities to move toward greater moral maturity and civic involvement. This tradition of practices inherited from an earlier time is our legacy, which we are beginning to reclaim.

Alexis de Tocqueville observed the "peculiar" American practice of being involved and of responding to the perceived needs of individuals and community: "Americans of all ages, all stations in life, and all types of disposition are forever forming associations. There are not only commercial and industrial associations in which all take part, but others of a thousand different types—religious, moral, serious, futile, very general and very limited, immensely large and very minute. Americans combine to give fêtes, found seminaries, build churches, distribute books, and send missionaries to antipodes. Hospitals, prisons, and schools take shape in that way. Finally, if they want to proclaim a truth or propagate some feeling by the encouragement of a great example, they form an association" (Tocqueville, [1830] 1969, p. 513).

Underlying much of the early voluntary activity in this country was the belief that the quality of community life was dependent on the moral character of its residents and that moral character was significantly shaped by one's participation and involvement in the community. This is a major premise of *Habits of the Heart,* in which Robert Bellah and his colleagues (1985, p. viii) write that "one of the keys to the survival of free institutions is the relationship between private and public life, the way in which citizens do, or do not, participate in the public sphere."

We participate in the public sphere primarily through voluntary activities, which range from short-term, time-limited events to longer-term commitments of service such as board membership. Involvement in events and the accomplishment of short-term tasks are necessary and valuable contributions to an organization. Such gifts of assistance can be of enormous help, whether it is in reaching important financial and program goals or through providing technical assistance. These acts create occasions in which community is created from sharing and working toward a common and attainable goal. Longer-term gifts of service involve not only the technical tasks but also developmental assistance in which the kind and complexity of relationships and responsibilities are substantively different. The choice to become a trustee of an organization is probably one of the most important decisions a volunteer will ever make and thus is deserving of careful thought. The choice to serve in the not-for-profit sector is an act of trusteeship, and when that choice is board membership, it is an act infused with historical significance and weight. Current recruitment and education efforts in board governance are being introduced to such historical connection as the context for service and leadership.

Accounts of early voluntary activities in this country say nothing about the education of volunteers. Their actions seemed to have evolved naturally from who volunteers saw themselves to be individually and corporately.

Analysis of what encouraged the service of early volunteers to others shows that it was the combination of several factors—primarily their religious beliefs, view of society, perception of community, view of the world, and, not least, will to survive. The early settlers' strong religious traditions, distrust of authority, and understanding of the need for cooperation in order to survive combined to foster concern for the common good and created the foundation for the later proliferation of voluntary associations. The early American psyche reflected an inseparable connection between the condition of the individual and the condition in the community. Survival needs may have dictated the high degree of consciousness about giving and caring early on, but they are not the sole explanation for the level of care and commitment that so many expressed and demonstrated. Their shared experience of oppression and persecution, the vision of creating a new order, the perception of a strong connection between beliefs and behavior and a culture that reinforced this, and the reality of being strangers in a strange land combined to create shared identity and community cohesiveness.

What can be done to retain the strengths of past practices for contemporary society? How can we better equip the not-for-profit sector that so strongly influences who we are and what we will become? How can we continue the legacy of trusteeship? A beginning answer is to invest in the recruitment and preparation of individuals who govern the not-for-profit sector.

The executive and program leaders in not-for-profits work in the hope of meeting the needs or others through institutional longevity; they sometimes work in tandem universes of what is and what is hoped for. Their day-to-day responsibilities must, of necessity, be focused on the here-and-now, but they experience the gravitational pull of the future on the present. The responsibility for determining the need for future existence and ensuring institutional longevity rests primarily with the governance leaders. They are entrusted with the existence of an organization: its past, present, and future. This level of responsibility requires education that includes preparation and development of leadership with the capacity to hold the institution in trust. It is a capacity at risk of being lost and that we will need to consciously work to reclaim.

Chapter Two

A Legacy in Jeopardy

The history of the not-for-profit sector links us to an important tradition and legacy of leadership and service in which individual interests and the common good coexist. Our sense of obligation for the common good is a definitive characteristic of American culture and is deeply ingrained in our being and behavior. Alexis de Tocqueville ([1830] 1969) marveled at the ways in which Americans cared for others and their capacity to engage in voluntary action for the common good. He also recognized another equally strong American characteristic—individualism—which he feared would eventually undermine the unique vitality of American voluntarism. His concern raised the question of whether the very wellspring of voluntary action contained the elements of its own demise.

Similar concerns and questions have surfaced in the writings of contemporary sociologists, philosophers, educators, and observers of leadership. One voice, Barry Schwartz (1986, p. 19), succinctly explains what is at risk of being lost: "In America, individualism was a matter of principle, a matter of right. But this individualism was tempered by several 'second languages' that united individuals and bound them together. These 'second languages'—one of religious conviction and one of civic virtue—were sources of moral tradition, of social mores, of 'habits of the heart.' They were what made it possible for people in pursuit of private, individual interests nevertheless to also share public communal purposes."

The demise of a shared moral language and set of practices that inspire a covenantal life of care and service can be attributed to the divisions between the public and private spheres of our lives. The separation of private and public, except in the sometimes bizarre forms of media confessionals, has created an isolationism in our individual and community lives that impoverishes not only our vocabulary but also our sense of connectedness. The fragmentation has at times led to self-centeredness and a withering of the common good. At a time when the health and stability of communities is at risk and our increased diversity is testing our capacity to cultivate the forces that foster the development both of self and community and of private and public life, the sense of a shared or common community has been diminished. Parker Palmer (1990, p. 30) aptly describes the adverse results of the split between the public and private realms: "The private has grown out of proportion in our society, and the inward journey has perverted into narcissism, partly because we have failed to identify their public counterweight."

The diminishment of individual and collective competence in managing the tension of the opposites and appropriately holding together the private and public realms is notable. Many are feeling a lack of adequate skills to cope with turbulent periods of transition and change. The state of anxiety in which we find ourselves has precipitated a quest for identity and meaning and has intensified the search for tools of control to provide some measure of adequacy and competence. It is clear that a major challenge we face is to manage change in ways that will be transformational. Returning to familiar patterns of behavior that give the illusion of being in control will not suffice. Without being equipped with an accurate reading of reality or having the capacity to deal with the stresses of rapid change and transitions, we may feel trapped, perceive few options, and operate in a survival rather than a creative mode. On boards, this can be manifested in denial and resistance to change or impulsive behavior, responses that are evident in the tendency toward quick decision making, intolerance of uncertainty, and scapegoating. Boards can break out of or avoid this behavioral cycle if they come to understand the consequences for their organizations and are given alternative ways to assume their responsibilities competently.

The majority of educational offerings for the development of boards are focused on administrative and management skills, strategic planning, and fundraising. Certainly these are important, but if they constitute the sole or primary approach to the formation of organizational governance and leadership, the board's capacity for perceiving and responding to complexity and its ability to engage in sustained contemplation of difficult issues, critical analysis, fore-sight, and thoughtful decision making may become insufficient.

Introducing volunteers to the responsibilities of governance only through the lens of management can narrow a board's leadership role. An obsession with issues of planning and organizing can narrow perceptions so that the visible and the objective become the sole determinants of reality, and people and organizations become divided, compartmentalized parts and pieces. The technical, managerial approach to board education is a valid one to introduce the responsibilities of governance that trustees need to have, but as boards begin to understand these technical tasks, their education needs to shift to an approach that focuses on the ability to lead through ambiguity and complexity, to see the origins and depth of problems and issues accurately, and to craft responses that can bring about appropriate changes in, if not radical transformation of, the institutions they serve. This is the educational discipline needed to increase a board's capacity to lead.

An overemphasis on individualism, the seeming demise of community, the loss of a language that expresses the gift relationship between individual and community, and the lack of consensus about the common good all contribute to the need for a new approach to the preparation and development of leadership for the not-for-profit sector. The current state of trusteeship development invites those of us who value the role of this sector to preserve the best of what citizen leaders can contribute to democracy, to value their contributions, to work to recover what is positive from the past, to develop educational concepts and practices for contemporary times, and to bridge divisions so that growing human needs can be met.

The cultivation of these capacities requires an intentional, depth education approach to board leadership—an approach in which specific tasks and activities are assigned to trustees and experienced in ways that connect them to a larger and greater purpose and work. Such a connection can be a mediating influence between self-interests and the common good, between individual mission and organizational purpose. When any one individual's mission is permitted to dominate a board, the connection to the larger context of organizational mission and purpose may be lost, and organizational decisions may be influenced more by individual charisma than organizational integrity.

With proper preparation and education for governance leadership, boards of trustees can continue the legacy of service and carry out the covenant "to care for each others' good and of the whole by everyone and so mutually" (Winthrop, 1965, p. 93). This can occur when there is a connection between the depths of an organization's culture and its practices. Leaders can engage in the habits of voluntary activity with an in-depth understanding of a historical tradition that retains the heart, nurtures voluntary involvement, and provides a purpose and a reason for being involved.

How can trustees be helped to respond more responsibly to the pull between self-interest and the common good in ways that lead to development of leaders with a deepened understanding of the relationship between individual character and the quality of community life? If the quality of our private lives contributes to the quality of community and the larger society, what do we need to foster in both the individual and community realms of our lives so that leaders can speak a language and engage in behavior that brings and binds people together in rich, dynamic ways? What is the modern equivalent of the 1620 Covenant—a new covenant that is reflective and respectful of our increased diversity, that will help us to reconnect and serve one another in new, life-giving ways?

The word *covenant* may be an uncomfortable word for some in the not-for-profit sector even though the very origin of many of these organizations is deeply covenantal. *Covenant* engenders a sense of community and invites shared responsibility, reciprocity, and generativity of gift. It opens up richer and deeper territory for understanding leadership, service, and community. Reclaiming, reinterpreting, and reintegrating the kind of language we use to describe the leadership in the not-for-profit sector can enable us to lead differently and provide a different kind of leadership education. If leadership could be viewed as covenantal in nature and in function, it might alter the ways we teach and practice it.

Parker Palmer (1990, p. 54) describes the concept of covenant and its significance to voluntary associations: "The covenant symbol is implicit, for example, in those voluntary associations still so central to American life—those little covenant groups where people join in a common commitment which however dimly it may reflect its origins, still links us to our covenantal past." When covenantal relationships are seen as the context for the practice of leadership, a very different leader and leadership education evolves. Covenantal relationships in voluntarism are an important legacy from the past and can serve as a way of exploring and defining current and future philanthropic practices.

Leadership is changing. How it is being defined and the ways in which it is being taught are being influenced by a number of variables that collectively influence our understanding. We are between two paradigms: one is a portrait of the past and the other a glimpse of our future. How we respond and adapt to them will be determined by our capacity to read the present accurately "with true hearts secure enough to face what is real" (Dykstra, 1994, p. 2). Table 2.1 sets out the fundamental shift in paradigms in terms of skills, style, knowledge, power, status, and structure in society— changes that are reshaping our views of leadership. We are moving from the scientific age paradigm into the relationship age. In reading current reality we can feel the in-between state and the experience of holding the tension of the opposites.

The scientific age reflects a paradigm of organizational and societal order and predictability that can be managed and monitored by the positional leader. The leader in such a structure operates as the ultimate source of power and authority. In contrast, in the relationship age leadership is perceived as something that is authorized by and negotiated with others. It relies on a structure that is nonhierarchical and flexible, dependent on many sources of authority to help complete tasks and attain goals. Both the scientific and relationship ages have strengths and limitations; the task of leadership is to view them as both-and rather than either-or. We are involved in a critical renegotiation of perspectives that will shape our capacity to respond to the present and the future. The goal is not to choose one paradigm over another, but to see and live with both long enough for the new to emerge. Creating hospitable space and reflective time to do this is important work. Activity—the filling up of time and space—is part of our reality, but if it is increasing too much, we can lose the ability to see what is really going on.

The very survival of our institutions hinges on the capacity of leaders to develop and maintain organizational cultures that foster and sustain autonomy and independence while strengthening the ability of individuals to care for and commit to the organization and the larger community. Leaders in the future will find it

**Table 2.1. A Shift in Paradigms:
The Context for the New Leadership**

	Scientific Age		*Relationship Age*
Skills:	Technical skills	↔	Adaptive skills
Style:	Command and control	↔	Invitation and interdependence
Methodology:	Competition	↔	Cooperation
Goal:	Gaining advantage	↔	Discerning purpose
Knowledge sought:	Gathering facts	↔	Finding meaning
Source of power:	What you have (wealth)	↔	What you know (information)
Structure:	Hierarchy (top-down)	↔	Circular (egalitarian)
Metaphor:	Machine (separate parts)	↔	Organic networks (connected parts)
Leadership:	Position	↔	Trusteeship

necessary to be able to read the larger environment at multiple levels and to know which levels to focus attention on if their organizations are going to negotiate change successfully.

Not-for-profit organizations need leaders who can engage in the practice of systemic thinking—the kind of thinking that brings a leader into direct contact and relationship with complexity, paradox, and ambiguity without being overwhelmed by confusion and despair. It is leadership that can comprehend the bigger picture without being pulled into tunnel vision or seduced by quick fixes. Reducing complexity to simplistic and concrete terms without working with the complexity and depth of issues does not lend itself to prophetic truth telling or accurate reality testing. Unless we can equip those in positions of trust with ways to deal effectively with the natural disorientation of change, we may be helping to sentence organizations to stagnation.

We must encourage the development of leadership education programs that value the practices of complex thinking and decision making. Trusteeship involves the exercise of these practices, and they can be cultivated and strengthened by trustees' acquiring comprehensive knowledge and engaging in in-depth analysis of the institutions served. This takes time and a level of intellectual engagement and commitment that is enriched by personal work and corporate reflection. There is a certain level of courage and wisdom that comes from developing the ability to explore deeper truths and levels of understanding of organizational life. There is a degree of trust and confidence established in the process that enables us to arrive at places that are respectful of the complexity of the organizations we serve.

We need to teach forms of education that prepare governance leaders to be prudent and to base decisions on knowledge born of a depth exploration and understanding of information, interpretation, and assignment of meaning, which leaves trustees with an understanding of their responsibility to hold the organization in trust. This kind of education gives significant and primary responsibility to trustees for the continuation of the organization's mission well beyond their tenure of service or their own existence. Acceptance of the responsibility to hold in trust is a gift that moves in a generative cycle, providing continuity of core essential values while aiding the organization in responsibly adapting to external changes.

The expectation that trustees hold an organization in trust requires them to move into an existing stream of history, which holds the potential for both continued progress and the demise of the organization. It is not a stream that remains still and unchanged or that can be ignored or underestimated. The degree to which trustees are aware and can move in and out of the stream of organizational history can be life enhancing or life threatening. In great part, the deciding factor that determines whether this movement is for good or ill is the leadership of the organization. Trustees can move much more flexibly and maneuver the rapids of change more facilely when they know the territory and the conditions affecting them and the organization. Such historical insight and preparation develops leaders who will be better able to manage change and transition.

Chapter Three

What Does It Mean to Hold in Trust?

The ability to hold someone or something in trust, to give to someone else or to give something of who we are and what we have, comes from our own experiences of being held in trust. Over time these experiences influence the development of certain beliefs and perceptions about our value and worth and the value and worth of others. The first is a belief that we are in relationship with and to others and that the stranger is a part of who we are and is a part of our world. This belief helps us to remember our common humanity and to perceive our differences as aspects of a whole rather than as disparate elements threatening our identity. When we see ourselves as being in relationship with and to one another, we can begin to embrace differences and be more creative in our efforts to connect and communicate with those who appear to be unlike us or who perceive things differently.

The second is a belief that something bigger and greater than self exists and that in some important way we belong to and are in service to a larger purpose. This belief helps us to have a broader, more communal view of a complex world and enables us to develop an ability to forgo impulsiveness and delay immediate gratification. The belief that we are tethered to something bigger than we are can embolden and encourage us and help us to face adversity.

To believe in something or someone greater than ourselves nurtures hope and purpose in our lives and gives meaning and purpose to the lives of others. Faith in the existence of something good and greater than ourselves, something transcendent, helps us to remember the significance of the spirit in our individual and corporate lives. We need more than mastery of techniques and tasks in leading and serving; we need the exploration of mystery, of the meaning of our lives and work. This may occur through religion, great books, ideas, relationships, conversation, art, music, and social movements. Whatever the source that inspires the journey, it can lead to a deep knowing that connects us and calls forth the giving of self.

The third belief is that giving transports us into a larger realm and into a cycle of generativity. We find ourselves members of a circle of ever increasing generosity from which abundance is created. In order to give to another, we must feel in possession of something to give. The acknowledgment of having something to give is an experience of abundance, and the sense of abundance helps to create conditions for the development and experience of community in which sharing with the stranger is part of the culture. Some of the most powerful times in our lives are when we have been genuinely and authentically given to by another individual who cares for us and in whom we have placed great trust. These are frequently persons who have had tremendous authority over us—for example, teachers, parents, friends, bosses, colleagues, or clergy. Our being cared for by them is an experience of being in a deeply mutual and respectful relationship—the experience of being held in trust.

The experience of being held in trust is one of being both vulnerable and empowered, of being uncertain and confident, of being guided through important life transitions and difficult life passages, and then emerging stronger and more integrated. Our capacity to give to and invest in someone or something else is seeded in relationships of trust holding. Our sense of self is conceived and subsequently shaped in these relationships of trust; this is where we learn who we are, where our perceptions of the world are formed and later redefined, and where our place in the world is revealed in time.

These initial and formative experiences teach us whether and how to trust. We take from our first caregiving relationships fundamental assumptions and beliefs about ourselves, others, and the external world. These assumptions and beliefs affect our perceptions, our capacity to form relationships, our interpretations of reality, our choices and actions. If we learned through experience that most people are responsible and trustworthy individuals and that all of us are

vulnerable to adversity sometime in life, our behavior toward someone going through difficult-times will be influenced by these perceptions. If we encounter a homeless stranger begging for money,
our response will likely be one of empathy and compassion with a
desire to alleviate the suffering in some way, whether through an immediate gift or some form of social advocacy or policy change. But
if our belief is that most people are irresponsible, untrustworthy individuals out to exploit others and looking for the easy answer, then
we will see the same situation with a different lens. The perception
of the homeless stranger might well be that of an irresponsible and
lazy street beggar whom we would be tempted to judge critically,
ignore, give advice to, or admonish.

Our beliefs indeed shape what we see and ultimately how we
behave. We draw conclusions from our experiences and apply them
to situations we encounter. In subtle and obvious ways, we are being
formed by what we are able to see.

New experiences and conscious choice can cause us to question,
challenge, and change our perceptions. Reflective analysis of our
past is an evocative and enlightening way we can come to know how
much of who we are now has been influenced by our experiences
with others. Michael, now an administrator in a large mental health
system, remembered a high school teacher who recognized his love
of music and encouraged him to persevere in mastering an instrument through an especially difficult time in his personal life. Never
pushy, the teacher gently urged him to persist and supported disci-
plined preparation and practice. Michael recalls, "There was never
a sense that I was being scripted or coerced into developing my artistic talents; instead I had a sense that something—something that
even I didn't fully know yet—was being called forth and being given
room and permission to grow." The practices inspired by this teacher
and in which he had engaged shaped Michael's love of music. The
discipline, focused passion, sense of responsibility, and joy this high
school teacher engendered within him remain with Michael today
and are reflected in his life and work. The teacher who held him in
trust helped to equip Michael to succeed as a supervisor of professional counselors who work with troubled individuals and as a high-
level administrator in a large mental health organization. Michael
realizes the influence he now has on the caregivers and on the system of health care. To him, his position is a way to give what was

given to him as a young adolescent: focused passion, discipline, responsibility, and joy. Being held in trust both enabled the growth of his capacity to hold in trust, and nurtured and obligated him to ensure the development of others who will share the capacity to hold in trust.

Holding someone or something in trust is a reminder of the significance of relationships and the value of self-discovery and definition in our lives. In the experience and exercise of trust holding, we are initiated into powerful streams of giving that move us along and strengthen and reinforce our responsibility to and for one another. Being held in trust prepares us for giving and introduces us to the reality of the other and the responsibility we have to come to know and embrace the stranger.

To come to know the stranger and the stranger's needs brings us to an awareness that there are needs beyond those of our own for which we have a responsibility and an obligation. When we can recognize and respond to the needs of another, we participate in a legacy of giving that recognizes the gift of receiving. We become the carriers of a legacy of abundance and generosity, a legacy initiated by and reinforced through practices of trust holding. The experience of being held in trust is one of being the recipient of a gift that needs to be shared with another. Preparation for trusteeship, whether of an individual or an organization, involves assisting them in the recovery of their experiences of giving and relationships of trust holding, and to connect these remembrances to their current responsibilities of governance leadership.

Leaders who hold others in trust are individuals who have been held in trust themselves; through their use of self and service, they have kept the gift given to them moving in ways that have enriched the development of other people, the performance of organizations, and the quality of community life. The capacity to hold in trust requires the sharing of self in a trustworthy manner so that the gift of service contributes not only to self-development but also to a greater good.

Becoming an independent, separate person, capable of establishing relationships of trust, functioning competently, seeing the complexity of life while retaining a core sense of self, and having a healthy sense of connection with something greater and larger than one's own being and of caring for others are the hallmarks of healthy adults. All of these qualities and abilities emanate from experiences of trust holding. When we have been the recipient of trust holding, we can understand both the value and limitations of individualism and the common good; perhaps more important, we are able to integrate rather than separate them. We can then better achieve a balance between them in our lives, our leadership, and our service to others.

A way to begin to identify and claim these capacities is through identifying the associations we have to the phrase "to hold in trust." When I have asked individual leaders and those with governance responsibilities to do this, their initial responses are halting but soon turn into a tumble of words, phrases, and images: "mentor . . . parent . . . supplicant hands . . . fiduciary . . . nurture . . . protect . . . commitment . . . balance . . . holding a candle . . . cradling a baby . . . holding a baby bird . . . believing . . . responsible for the future . . . accountable . . . stewardship . . . integrity . . . security . . . for the future . . . continuity . . . caring . . . parenting . . . involved . . . patience . . . authentic . . . dependable . . . courage . . . love . . . respect . . . confidence . . . knowledgeable . . . compassionate . . . challenged to do the best . . . seeing the unrealized potential in me." These words and phrases are doorways to personal stories that collectively provide a verbal portrait and a terrain of trust from which individual character is formed. Participants are asked to recall a time when they were held in trust and to answer several questions: Who held you in trust? What did they do? How were you affected by what they did? By who they were? What were the qualities and characteristics of those who held you in trust? After some time for individual reflection, participants gather in small groups to share the answers to these questions. Later in whole group discussion, I typically ask if they now have other associations to "hold in trust," and what appeared to be a comprehensive list expands to include new words, phrases, and associations that convey the more deeply personal and relational aspects of having been held in trust.

Susan, a woman in her early forties, recalled her relationship with her mother, who strongly believed in Susan's abilities even as Susan doubted them. As a young adolescent, she approached leadership and service opportunities with reticence, but her mother's quiet yet persistent confidence in her provided Susan with a safe emotional space to risk trying new things. Susan recounted numerous projects she took on with her mother's blessings and belief she could do it. Over time the trust her mother had in her took root and grew. Her desire to do for others became her own, and the opportunities given to her seeded her own passion to make sure that other young women have opportunities to succeed. Susan is a now a staff member and leader in an organization dedicated to this end. The trust holding she received as a young girl is now a gift she gives to her colleagues, board members, program staff, and the young women served by her organization.

This story is an example of how the experience of being held in trust can be the inception of a calling and can influence important life choices. A colleague, Jim, speaks eloquently of a treasured friendship that began in adolescence with a family friend and businessman who became a priest later in life. This friend was someone with whom Jim could share his hopes and concerns, his aspirations and fears. It was this friend who enabled Jim to call forth his deep yearning for a life of service to God and to discern his calling to be a priest in the Episcopal church. Jim served in several positions before becoming the rector of a prominent urban parish, where he remained for nearly twenty years. During his tenure, he created a community of worship and spiritual nurture for many accomplished community leaders who were seeking meaningful and responsible ways to serve the greater community. His experience of being held in trust not only evoked Jim's own calling but enabled him to help others to determine and express their vocations. Jim is now the leader of a theological institution whose mission is the preparation of clergy and lay leadership.

Recalling times of being held in trust can be an emotionally powerful experience; we are reminded of a time when someone accepted, understood, and cared enough about us to invest of themselves, their time, and other resources and enabled us to reach new levels in our personal and professional lives. The remembrance of these relationships brings forth a sense of thankfulness and gratitude for the gift received, and the gratitude brings with it the sense of obligation to give back to others. It calls forth a sense of duty that is absent of debilitating "shoulds and ought to's" that originate from a sense of scarcity. To live as though we are truly connected to and in relationship with strangers creates a very different sense of responsibility and community. From this connection we learn that accountability brings freedom and that loss and sacrifice bring renewal and growth.

Effective trusteeship blends caring and competence, connects altruism and authority, and evolves from the generous act of being held in trust—the experience of being given to. Being held in trust is a profoundly personal experience that shapes individual and organizational character and behavior. In the cycle of giving, its influence is felt collectively and culturally. Institutional and personal exploration of what it means to be held in trust and to hold in trust helps those who assume a position of leadership in the not-for-profit sector to make important connections between the private and public realms of life, and to lead with integrity and authenticity.

Chapter Four

Preparing for Trusteeship

The development of trustee leadership begins with a discernment of individual connection and commitment to the historical identity and mission of an organization. Accomplishing this includes an examination and clarification of individual motivations for choosing to serve and for assuming the responsibility of governing an institution. An understanding of what attracts us to serve and to lead an organization, of what motivates us to become a member of the board, of what causes us to care deeply about the future of the organization, and of what helps us to remain active and committed is vitally important knowledge for staff who are focused in the present while laboring toward a vision of the future. It is also vital information for the board whose responsibility it is to determine the current and future welfare of the organization.

We can begin the process of discernment with questions. What is it that calls me to this work? To this particular place? At this specific time? What do I expect? What is expected of me? What do I find joy in doing? All of these questions are pathways to leadership formation. Our personal motivation and sense of calling are areas of our lives that are frequently presumed too private to broach, and therefore deemed off-limits in conversations in which individuals are being recruited for board service. There are few resources available to help potential board members pose these kinds of questions or ferret out the answers to them. And if we operate in the belief that there is not time to ask more than perfunctory questions of candidates for governance leadership, we will lack the information needed to make the best match between character and capability and between individual interests and organizational needs. Making time for a depth conversation with potential board members about their values and their vision, what they care deeply about, and why and how they want to contribute and make a difference will help you examine character and commitment on a level that cannot be gleaned from a chronological listing of positions and achievements on résumés or application forms.

This was an unforgettable learning in an organization providing programs for women in impoverished conditions. The organization had attracted a prominent and predominantly male board. Those who deemed the board's composition highly unusual for this type of organization found through an examination of members' individual histories that the common reason for their commitment was that their mothers or other relatives had helped to found the organization. As children these men had been involved in their mothers' voluntary service to the organization. Their introduction to and education for public service had occurred literally at their mothers' knees, and their capacity to invest was deeply rooted in a personal connection to its history. In a significant way, each felt he was doing what important family members had always done and that he was also carrying forth a legacy that was familial and organizational. Their depth conversation and education occurred over time through personal relationship and service inspired by family commitment. The influence of personal connections to organizational mission and to choices in voluntary action can be powerful, as this story of board members demonstrates.

Organizations want leaders who are good at what they do (competent) and who are also caring and good people (character). Yet we sometimes have difficulty combining competence and character when we recruit and prepare governance leaders. One of the reasons for this difficulty is a disconnect between what we do and who we are that affects the quality of community and institutional life. Being and doing have been splintered, with performance emphasized over personhood. Yet the legacy of trusteeship is one in which being and doing coexist. They are not broken apart into an either-or dichotomy but brought together in a paradoxical state of both-and. This is the legacy of trusteeship that prepares boards to engage in the adaptive work of leadership (Heifetz, 1994). It is work that claims the need for individual achievement while also enabling collective accomplishment; it is the work of developing both self and community, of giving and receiving.

Engaging leaders in a process of self-discernment and discussions of historical tradition, organizational ethics, and personal values can foster the development of being and doing, which when integrated fosters trustworthy leadership. Disconnections between being and doing can diminish organizational capacity to carry out mission. One example is a prestigious women's group whose primary activities centered on community service, youth projects, and the development of a cohesive, supportive community for professional women. When the group's board became engaged in a divisive campaign over the election of its next president, the acrimonious debate and politicization of the process split the board and carried the conflict over into the larger membership. The founders of the group anguished over the conflict. The polished, professional demeanors that many manifested in their daily jobs were not in evidence; objectivity of information had been lost, and individuals were absorbed into the conflict at a very personal level. Those members who attempted to examine the reasons for this fractious behavior found that they were personally attacked.

The external behavior of the organization was incompatible with its being. Board members had a lapse in their memory of what they had been asked to hold in trust when they agreed to serve on the board. The questions of organizational history and identity had not been raised, and communication about the conflicts had no other framing than that of a personal context. If the board had been able to see that it was out of sync with its historical character (being), it would have been able to see the incongruence of its actions (doing). The divisive conflict over who should lead the organization was symptomatic of a subterranean and unresolved issue of whom the group deemed acceptable for membership, an issue connected to the group's very origins and identity. The decision over the choice of leadership touched off a deeper question of acceptability—one that lurks in the culture of every group: Who is included and who is excluded?

A later examination of the organization's membership policies revealed that the group's recruitment policies were incongruent with its practices. The stated policies framed from its inception were inclusive, but the recruitment practices had been exclusive. The disconnection between the organization's stated values and its actual practices had helped to create the dis-ease and the subsequent explosions. The incongruence became personalized, but its origins were were discovered to be an institutional amnesia that permitted a split between being and doing.

Eventually a new president was elected, prompting a number of members to resign. The loss of many strong leaders was detrimental to the group, but what may be as damaging is the unresolved understanding of the conflict, which if left unexamined may exact a high price during the next significant transition in the organization's life. This experience is now woven within the fabric of the organization's history, and the memory of what occurred is embedded at some deeper level. Part of the organization's current history is a diminishment of trust and damaged relationships that will undermine the organization's ability to manage future conflict and damage its vitality if they are not addressed.

If the conflict over the choice of a leader had been perceived as an indicator of organizational incongruence, it could have been handled by reexamining the core beliefs and values of the organization and how they fit with its actions. Had such an examination occurred, a discussion about how to align them might have followed. Such an approach would have generated more options and provided a wider range of choices from which an acceptable decision about leadership could be made.

The separation of being from doing always carries a price. It can prevent the work of periodically plowing the soil of organizational beliefs and values; when this occurs, new seeds of growth lie fallow. The disconnect between doing and being costs us our humanness and reduces the capacity to tolerate ambiguity and respond to change responsibly. When we permit the division between being and doing, it becomes easier to rationalize behavior that is inconsistent with who we say we are. Programs and services can become self-absorbed and insular, out of touch with the needs and interests of those they are intended to serve. Perhaps the ultimate danger to us as individuals is a disconnection from those far different than we are. When we are out of touch with or lack reverence for our whole being, it is difficult to see differences or to revere them. The separation at this level can cast a shadow so deep and wide that those with whom we work and those who are the recipients of our services can be eclipsed by it. We literally cannot see. The capacity to take in the full picture of another human or the person's environment is marred unless we find the courage to risk encountering our own inner being. This is the work that helps us to claim our gifts and limitations, and claiming them eradicates the need to make others carry them for us. It is deep work—inner work.

Inner work brings us into contact with the shadow: a place where aspects of our selves that we are not ready to accept are cloistered. Depending on our capacity to face them, they can become either avenues or obstacles to future growth or development. This is not easy work. It is difficult to talk about, especially in an environment that doubts or denies its existence and has left us uneasy about such a notion as an inner life. We live with this part of ourselves daily as individuals and as members of groups and systems. Overreactions, personalization of conflict, the need to diminish others, sabotage, love of palace intrigue, destructive gossip, and passive-aggressive behavior are all symptomatic of unfinished inner work. All are highly costly to any relationship and organization.

Resistance to the existence of shadow in individual life and organizational culture can build up forceful reservoirs of feeling; when they are triggered, they can feel overpowering and out of control. These sometimes threatening and emotional explosions can reinforce fears about dealing with this part of ourselves or of an organization. So some of the resistance to inner work or shadow work is understandable until we can understand the paradox that to engage in this work reduces the risks of conflict and dissension, and avoiding it creates the very difficulties with which we are uncomfortable. Acknowledging and analyzing the shadow in individual leadership and organizational life is transformative. It is useful to explore the depths of the relationship between our being and our doing and the effect they have on the leadership and service we provide to organizations and communities. Addressing these issues in leadership education provides a great service that can aid organizations in better preparation of volunteers for trusteeship.

One example of what can occur when this work is done is an event in the life of a prominent half-century-old religious institution. The executive director and board president of the organization expressed grave concern at a board meeting over a financial shortfall. The discussion led to their requesting assistance in long-range planning. The executive director was the fourth person to hold the position and had already served four years. Her predecessor had been persuaded to leave after a ten-year tenure because board leaders felt the organization's educational offerings had declined in quality and appeal. No assessment of the reasons for decline had been done at the time (other than speculation), and although the organization experienced a minor upsurge in registrations the following year, attendance reverted to previous levels and was suffering a slow, steady decline at the time the organization requested help.

As preparation began to help the board engage in strategic planning, pervasive distrust between the executive director and the board president was noted. All of the reasons for this situation were not apparent, but one major reason seemed to be a lack of clarity about each one's specific role and set of responsibilities. The executive director cited several instances in which she felt her authority with staff had been undermined by the board president's inappropriate interventions in day-to-day operations. No resolution of these problems had occurred, and the resultant feelings of both the director and the president infected every communication or transaction between them. This relationship made it difficult for the staff and board to communicate with optimum clarity or accuracy of information because their interaction was so colored by old baggage. The strong emotions bankrolled from the past made it difficult for either one to listen to the other with care. Past unresolved conflicts kept getting in the way of the work that needed to be done. Until they acknowledged and dealt with these difficulties directly, substantive progress could not occur. An intervention was designed to help the organization's staff and trustees examine themselves at both the personal and organizational levels. As the emotional smoke cleared, it was easier for them to see what was their work and what was the organization's work.

It is important to help organizations in this kind of situation work simultaneously on being and doing—on the internal and external issues. The challenge is to not get bogged down in either dimension, but to work to reintegrate them so that the leaders of an organization can operate from a basis of health and integrity. When a group is able to accomplish this degree of integration between being and doing, the sense of group cohesion, trust, and accomplishment grows.

Theoretically, recruitment for board service begins with an assessment of what the board and the organization need followed by the generation of a list of people who could potentially meet these needs. Because it is important to have trustees with influence and credibility and who by their external accomplishments are judged as able and suited for the responsibility, there is a strong tendency to select those who have recognizable status and position within the community. Much of an organization's survival depends on its reserve of public trust; the caliber of trustees can be a sign of legitimacy and a litmus test of community support. And assumptions about the quality of the organization are often made based on the governance leaders that an organization attracts. It is therefore understandable that most board selection processes focus on aspects of individual visibility, public persona, title, degrees, financial resources, and individual expertise and known skills. This is important information to consider in developing a governance group. Nevertheless, more and different information is needed. Obtaining it is time-consuming, however, and more personal than we typically are comfortable with being.

Getting more and different information challenges those strongly held beliefs or practices that the personal and professional realms need to be kept separate. What is essential for staff and board members to know, when we think of them as being much too busy to take time for personal reflection and discernment in their voluntary lives? This is a challenging question every organization needs to ask as it seeks to prepare volunteers for governance leadership. Sometimes not knowing much about an organization whose board one serves on can lead to a values clash. This was observed during one board retreat when a lively discussion of the organization's mission triggered considerable emotion in one male member. He was quite perturbed because he thought that one of the stated values of the organization sounded "too much like women's lib!" The retreat was the first time that he had heard that the primary reason for the existence of the organization was to be an advocate for equal opportunities for girls. No one had inquired about his beliefs or values concerning the role of females in society before he was invited to join the board, and there had not been an opportunity to see if there was a connection joining his personal beliefs, professional expertise, and the organization's mission.

The real issue may not be how busy the volunteers whom we ask to serve on boards are, but whether we can instill in them the value of discernment, of revealing personal values and beliefs, and of applying them to the decision to serve and lead an organization.

Most volunteers who serve on boards want to contribute competently and achieve constructive and enduring results. They also have a host of other claims competing for their time. Not-for-profits can help these volunteers become more conscious of their motivation for service and encourage reflection on their internal and external lives to help them develop criteria for deciding to commit to board service.

The syndrome of the overextended, busy volunteer is a pervasive one—one we can permit to perpetuate the perception of scarcity and limitation and the belief that busy volunteers do not have time for more than brief episodes of education. New ways of seeing and being a board and of carrying out the roles and responsibilities of governance may be difficult to maintain in such a climate of resistance, typically characterized by such plaintive comments as these: "My board doesn't want to ponder these kind of questions." "We can only meet for an hour and a half to work on the mission." "No one will take a day and a half to plan." "Can't you do something in a half-day? That's as long as I can get them to stay."

The belief that the governance leaders of an organization do not have the time to receive a depth education encourages a situation in which the organization's staff assumes the responsibilities of governance and are reluctant to transfer them to the board. Staff are co–trust holders in an organization and share this responsibility through their service to clients, providing effective programs that meet client needs and helping to develop policies and future direction. Once staff become accustomed to operating as the governance trustees of an organization, they find it quite difficult to give this responsibility back to the board, especially if the board lacks comprehensive knowledge of the organization and does not know what it means to hold it in trust. Many administrative and program staff whisper in private their concerns about their board's true ability to serve the organization while publicly perpetuating the perception that their boards are highly functioning governance bodies. Governance leadership is hard work when it is done right and done well. Every board member will not be able to assume the needed level of responsibility, and when they cannot, this can be constructively acknowledged.

One of the most effective ways this can occur is through a board retreat in which the organization's culture, core values and beliefs, its mission and vision are shared, followed by a discussion of what kind of board is necessary to hold the organization in trust. This presents an opportunity to set the standards and expectations for governance leadership and to have each board member determine if and how they are meeting them. The majority of members want to meet the expectations, but if it becomes clear to some of them that they aren't going to be able to, they can choose to leave. In our experience this leave taking is done without anger or blame, but rather with a strong belief that the organization deserves better than what they are presently able to give. This manner of leaving can be an act of trusteeship.

The impact on organizations that operate under the assumption that accomplished professionals who volunteer for board service automatically know what it means to be a trustee needs to be seriously considered. Accomplishment in professional endeavors is not an automatic credential for trusteeship. I have been told numerous times that chief executive officers of successful companies who are recruited for not-for-profit board service would be insulted if they were told they needed board education. Yet if they were told the truth during recruitment about the responsibility they have assumed, they would understand the need for it. Board members should be brought into an organization in ways that communicate to them that their involvement is so important that the organization is investing in their education. A board member is a partner in a dynamic enterprise, not an interchangeable part in a machine. "Not-for-profit" is a descriptor that does not automatically convey the rich diversity of organizations; those who hold organizations in trust need to be knowledgeable about the particularity of the organization they serve.

In some of the workshops I conduct, participants are asked to recall their first experience of being asked to serve on a board. The story typically recounted is some variation of the following conversation:

Board member: Hello, John. This is Susan. How are you?
Prospective board member: Hi, Susan. Other than being a little too busy, I'm fine. How about you?

Board member: Great! It's been pretty busy here too, but we're doing well. I'm so glad I caught you. I serve on the board of XYZ organization, an organization I feel is doing some really good things. We work with young adolescent boys and girls in Bond County. Last year we worked with over twelve hundred young people through tutoring services, camp activities, and counseling programs. Every year we sponsor the Arts Auction Gala, where we raise about $60,000. Most of our budget comes from the United Way, individual contributions, foundation grants, and corporate donations. We are in the middle of a capital campaign to raise money for the completion of our new career center. You can see that these are exciting and challenging times for us.

Prospective board member: It certainly sounds like a lot is going on.

Board member: Yes, and one of them is that we are in the process of nominating new board members. I'm calling to invite you to join the XYZ Board. I think you would be a great addition. You and I worked so well together on the Children's Benefit for the Youth Guild last year. Your financial acumen would help us out a lot.

Prospective board member: Thank you. I'm very flattered to be asked, but I'm not sure if I have the time. I've been asked to chair the Readmore Project for the Boys' Center next year. So . . .

Board member: Wonderful! I've heard about that project, but really what I'm asking you to do won't take up too much of your time. The board meets once a month for an hour and a half on the second Tuesday at noon. The lunches are great! You would be on a committee of your choice. You would be such an asset. I know your organizing and fundraising skills will be a big help to XYZ.

Prospective board member: Well, thank you for your vote of confidence. I'd like to be of help. If I don't have to attend every meeting, it sounds doable.

Board member: You could miss a couple before you run into difficulty. This is wonderful! You'll see what a first-rate program and staff we have, and the board is a great bunch of people. You'll fit right in. We'll send you a letter after our meeting this month confirming your appointment as a board member. The next meeting is the fifteenth of the month at noon. We'll send you a notice. I look forward to seeing you! Thanks again. Good-bye.

Prospective board member: You're welcome. Good-bye.

Some version of this conversation happens to many new board recruits across the country; they commit to board membership with a similar level of information exchange. Of course, the individuals being asked to serve are known and recommended by someone who currently serves on the organization's board, and some criteria for selection have probably been used. Boards generally take seriously the responsibility of replenishing their membership. Gaps in knowledge about the organization can be remedied later at an orientation session in which those new to the organization are given thick, three-ring binders that contain copies of the organization's articles of incorporation, by-laws, a mission statement, the budget, a roster of members, the board minutes and committee structure, a schedule of meetings, and committee assignments. The sheer volume of information and the form in which it is presented to a new trustee can be quite overwhelming. Yet in addition to this stack, the newest members of a board need to be given a clear sense of the true character and calling of this particular organization, of its priorities, and of what they as trustees need to attend to most and first among the myriad of issues and concerns identified. At the point of orientation, the ties that connect new board members to an organization are not as strong as they will become. Until those bonds are well established, the natural tendency during this early stage is to look to other board members for guidance and direction in decision making. It is an act of trust and dependency of which the more experienced board members need to be reminded. New board members need to be encouraged to exercise their voices so that the group process does not become groupthink.

The information contained in board orientation manuals is important. Board members need to be introduced to the content in ways that can ensure that it will be remembered and useful. The stages of recruitment and orientation of board members are optimal teaching moments in an organization. The attention normally paid to the management and administrative elements of governance can be expanded to include those of trusteeship and elements of depth education. The critical issues—organizational identity and character, the volunteer as a trust holder, the importance of possessing a passion for the mission of the organization, the value of having clarity of purpose and dedication to service, the significance of having a fit between organizational purpose and behavior, the importance of attending to the culture of the board as well as that of the organization—can all be introduced at a time when they are most needed and likely to be remembered.

A workshop exercise that can be used for both seasoned and new trustees demonstrates how the value of early preparation for the exercise of trusteeship can be emphasized to board members. Each person is asked to pair up with someone he or she has just met and plan each other's lives for the next year. A number of the participants are skilled in planning; many have been quite successful in their work and are proficient at setting and accomplishing goals. They are told that they have twenty to thirty minutes to complete this task. After briefly hesitating, they immediately plunge into the activity, and in spite of any initial discomfort and hesitation, each person develops a plan for the individual he or she has just met. Although they experience mild anxiety and an initial tentativeness, their ample skills kick in, and they complete the task. Although the end products possess the essential features of good plans, something is missing. It is in the recognition of this incompleteness that an understanding emerges of the reasons for the initial uneasiness they experienced in doing the assignment. What is missing is a depth of knowledge and understanding of the individual for whom the plan is intended. A generic approach to planning may be harmless, but it may not be helpful because it lacks a solid knowledge of the subject. The plan, even when completed, lacks the ingredients for it to be trusted.

The lessons from this brief exercise parallel what many describe as their first experience of joining a board. With minimal knowledge, they find themselves in a position in which critical decisions about the life and future of the organization must be made. They enter into an arena of decision making with notable skills; they are adept at strategic planning and capable of assisting the organization in the development of a finished plan of action. Whether these impressive skills result in an appropriate plan for a particular organization is the key question, and it is even more pertinent to ask in these circumstances. The process of effective, ethical planning and decision making for an organization requires an ability to distinguish the board's role between "doing things right" and "doing the right thing" in the process (Bennis and Nanus, 1985, p. 21). Trustees are responsible for the exercise of both management and leadership, balancing pragmatism with passion and technical skills with problem solving. When all the elements on each of these continua are considered, the community can be assured that those who occupy such special positions of public trust are equipped to carry out their responsibilities.

Time does need to be considered in the preparation and education of trustees. Resources such as time are not unlimited, and there is a considerable range of choices about its use that can be made. When the perception is that time is tight and board members are overextended, there is a corresponding tendency to become more dependent on the known and the familiar. Management responsibilities and skills are more familiar territory, and when there are time constraints, many organizations focus on management competencies in the search for and preparation of board members. The resulting limitation of focusing too much on management skills is well described by Robert Greenleaf (1996, pp. 221–223): "There is an occupational disability in the managerial craft that limits able managers in generating those visions which are absolutely essential for providing a sense of purpose and direction in the institution. . . . The managerial mind is limited by its first priority to get things done in the immediate situation, and to keep the institution afloat from day-to-day. To get things done one must concentrate on the short range. The long range, the indefinite future framed in a good view of the distant past, requires a different kind of thinking."

The consequences of focusing solely or primarily on management are that we prepare board members to think more in the short term and cultivate acting in the moment at the expense of developing the capacity for thoughtful contemplation and reflection about the distant future. Those who serve as trustees of institutions can be prepared for a new perspective that can lead to a holistic, integrated view of organizations and a new understanding of what is required for the board to lead.

A broader view of the role of trustees that includes management skills and creates a space in which board members can rediscover their historical connections to the legacy of voluntary service found throughout the "founding and formative" stories of not-for-profit organizations and the larger context of philanthropic history is excellent preparation for trusteeship. Peter Dobkin Hall (1992, p. 9) describes the transformative effect a broader view can have on individuals and the larger society:

> In contrast to the third sector's view of itself, which has tended to stress the importance of the professionalization of management and to marginalize the role of the board of trustees—which are increasingly composed of professional men and women of diverse backgrounds, rather than the WASP [white Anglo-Saxon Protestant] males who once dominated them—the vision of the possibilities of the third sector embraced by the "knowledge workers" is a far broader and more hopeful one. For the former, the purposes (mission) of an organization is the product of efficient management; for the latter, efficiency is merely a means of realizing organizational purposes. On the face of it, the differences may seem minor. But in a setting in which the survival of society itself will depend on its ability to optimize the willing and committed participation of all relevant stakeholders, it is the difference between defining the stewardship responsibilities of trustees narrowly—as fiduciary oversight of a particular organization—or broadly—as representing the interests of society as a whole. The former leads trustees toward policies in

which the organization's survival is paramount; the latter, toward policies in which the good of the organization is considered in relation to, not apart from, the good of society.

Contemporary social conditions and the complex nature of change itself mandate thoughtful and conscientious approaches to the development of those who serve our communities and lead in all sectors, especially in the not-for-profit sector. These conditions and the needs of the not-for-profit sector necessitate a new educational approach to leadership development. The development of leadership able to articulate a vision that captures our imagination about what we can be and provide practices and the discipline to achieve it will take a considerable investment of time and patience. How we perceive and define the responsibilities of trusteeship will have a profound effect on our organizations and communities. The definition and the practices that express it become a framework for development of a way of integrating being and doing, of bridging and balancing the public and the private, and creating a more civil society.

In the early years of this country's formation, what appeared to be altruistic behavior—the capacity to care for others—was shaped by a particular culture and reinforced by a set of practices that integrated the personal and public realms of people's lives. The character of individuals grew out of the soil and soul of a societal culture called to "care for each other's good and the whole by everyone and so mutually" (Ellis and Noyes, 1990, p. 18), and through culturally sanctioned practices these words were made real. Serving others was an explicit norm established and lived out in community practices. The character of institutions mattered because they were perceived as places for the nurturance and formation of individuals. The being and character of those who created these places mattered.

Societal fragmentation and divisiveness in contemporary society challenge us to recover the best of the past, to recover the legacy of trusteeship if we have a stake in our future as a nation and as a people. We can be more conscious about the preparation of individuals for service and leadership and ensure that the best traditions of civic responsibility and public service continue. Fears about the crumbling of organizational and societal infrastructure will not lead to panic or despair if they are seen as indicators of the need to look for new ways to prepare citizens for service and leadership.

Chapter Five

A Framework for Understanding Trusteeship

Volunteers in the not-for-profit sector can benefit from a different and more comprehensive preparation in order to assume the responsibilities of trusteeship: combining competence with compassion and connecting personal mission to the mission of the organization. The ability to see these connections and relationships is fundamental to the development of effective trusteeship. A depth approach to the education of individuals and organizations is particularly helpful if it can demonstrate and strengthen these connections. An examination of the relationship between altruism and authority is useful in this regard. The combination of these elements exists in varying degrees within each of us; the form their behavioral expression takes is influenced by the times and situations in which we find ourselves.

Altruism means caring for the welfare of others; it is the ability to be concerned about the condition or state of being of another human and to acknowledge and meet the needs of that other. It is embodied in and through countless acts of service to others every day and is most effective when giving is based on the needs of the recipients. It is multidimensional giving of self, time, money, skills, talents, and so on. The giving is out of a depth of understanding and compassion for the other. It is relational and predicated on a belief in the dignity and worth of people and in their capacity to be capable, responsible individuals.

In contemporary times, the exercise of serving is frequently limited to immediate and short-lived activities. Altruism, however, is the sustained exercise of serving over time, of being committed to something beyond one's own self and inner circle, of serving in a manner that will likely have a transformative effect on both the giver and the recipients of the gift.

Altruism raises the issue of motivation and provides an ethical standard for acts of service. Why do we want to help someone else? Why would a person care about a small, struggling social service agency? Why do we raise funds for numerous causes? Why do we think we can make the world a better place? The answers are connected to who we see ourselves to be, how we believe we are related to the world, and our perceptions of individual and communal value identity. Altruism is located in the very being of the individual involved and encountered in his or her expressions of serving.

Authority is the degree of power accorded to, vested in, and exercised by an individual, organization, or group in order to perform functions deemed important to those over which the authority is exercised. It is person centered yet communally shaped. The basis of authority might be positional, legal, or experience based, or it might stem from competence, relationships, or tradition. Those with authority recognize its role in their interactions and transactions and its use in the creation of change.

Effective leadership integrates altruism and authority. It is an integration that evokes the moral and ethical use of power and authority through position, knowledge, and skills to bring about changes in the well-being of individuals, institutions, and communities. This approach is respectful of the need for individual interests yet also considerate of the common good. It requires an ability to maintain a view of the complexity of problems and issues while exercising the capacity to respond responsibly in ambiguous, sometimes conflictual situations without being overwhelmed by despair, overcome by impulsiveness, or driven to inflexibility. The leader's perspective is wider, even in situations that require focus and immediate action. The choice to act is contextually and communally influenced, and is considerate of more than any one individual or any one issue. The leader lives in and operates out of a world of multilayered complexity, sharing a particular view and interpreting the experience in compelling ways that enables others to develop trust and to risk being and doing.

People manifest these capabilities in an infinite variety of ways and in a multitude of situations. When altruism and authority are optimally combined in the practice of trusteeship, the effect is transformational in all the spheres of life. It ushers in change encircled by a sense of the common good and considerate of individual interests. There are four combinations of altruism and authority that affect the work and practice of developing trustee leaders (see Figure 5.1).

Marginals

Individuals who have little altruism, minimal understanding of the concerns and needs of others, and a weak sense of internal and external authority do not exercise leadership and are often at the fringes of the core activities of the organization. Marginals, as they are called, are unlikely to seek volunteer responsibilities requiring long-term commitment or sustained investment of time and self. They lack a sense of connection to or responsibility for strangers or for things outside of their personal sphere. They are either unaware

Figure 5.1. Altruism/Authority Leadership Model

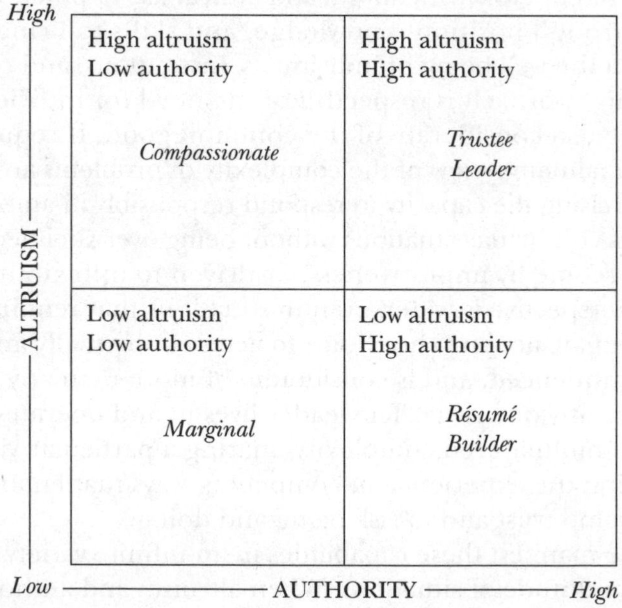

High altruism Low authority *Compassionate*	High altruism High authority *Trustee Leader*
Low altruism Low authority *Marginal*	Low altruism High authority *Résumé Builder*

ALTRUISM (vertical axis: Low to High)

AUTHORITY (horizontal axis: Low to High)

or only minimally comprehend that there is something bigger than themselves or that they have a circle of influence. Out of insularity derived from either privilege or deprivation, they become cocooned within a social narcissism that is isolating and narrowing.

There are several possible explanations as to why an organization would have a Marginal board member. It might be because the person represents a constituency served or has access to or possesses wealth. The organization may have an immediate and specific need that this individual has the resources to address and solve. Whatever the specific reason for this person's joining the board, his or her authority is derived from external position rather than from altruism.

Marginals may be perceived as deadwood on a board if they do not appear to be contributing much in meetings, do not follow through on responsibilities, and seem to have no more than passing interest in the issues being discussed. As one colleague, a seasoned gardener, reminded me, "Deadwood is full of life and nutrients that can aid in the growth of other organisms." Certainly individuals who fall within this quadrant have the potential to make valuable contributions to an organization, but if their participation in the organization is allowed to remain narrow in focus and their services primarily technical and concrete, their ability to affect the long-term health of the organization will be compromised. And their own development will be thwarted.

The Marginal's primary motivation for participation in voluntary organizations is social connections to other members rather than synchronicity with the organization's overarching mission. They support individual activities yet end up being sealed off from the core of the organization's reason for existing, which could instead infuse and invigorate their service. If an organization has too many board members that fit this category or if one individual like this decides to drive the agenda, their influence could be damaging to the organization in the long term.

If an individual influences decisions on a board because of position or possessions rather than knowledge of the organization and a commitment to its mission, the governance group risks becoming self-serving and focused on issues and events that meet the board members' needs. If this happens, decisions tend to be made for the members' immediate gratification and benefit rather than for the good of the organization. An example illustrates how this can happen.

At an annual retreat of a board of an organization responsible for school reform, the members struggled with the question of how their program could effect improvement in the quality of teaching in the schools. It was clearly a tough issue, and the conversation was interlaced with uncomfortable silence. As facets of the issue unfolded, some group members began to address the relevance of the organization's mission and pose questions: Can it be the job of a voluntary organization that is external to the school system to affect the quality of teaching? Should we focus our work on providing resources for educators? As the level of discomfort increased in the group, ideas to solve the problem were offered at an increasing frequency. Yet the potential solutions seemed only to raise the levels of anxiety and frustration in the group because no one seemed to have a clear definition of the problem they were trying to solve.

At this point in the discussion, a highly placed positional leader in the community recommended that the board plan and execute a public relations event, "selling" the organization and making it more visible to the community at large. He argued that greater visibility would help the organization's fundraising in the future. He also suggested the group sponsor a parade close to the start of the school year "to get the community's attention." The group responded with silence—a silence that conveyed a sense of being diverted from the direction in which they felt they needed to go. Nevertheless, no one challenged the idea, and the silence was accepted as consent. Soon after this meeting, the group planned the proposed event. The experience was fun for most of the group, but it did not capture the community's attention or generate the support hoped for, and it did little to convey to the community the mission and vision of the organization.

Sometimes marketing events can galvanize community support and initiate a valuable public ritual and dialogue that coheres the issues and galvanizes community action. This particular suggestion, however, lacked a more comprehensive understanding of what the organization was facing, and it failed to consider a purpose greater than the board members' own interests. There must be substance attached to ritual and symbolism; otherwise there is a superficiality and shallowness of spirit that hovers over activities and programs.

A public relations campaign under the circumstances seemed more an act of self-promotion than an act of trusteeship on behalf of public education or the community at large. If this group had centered the conversation on its mission, it might have been able to generate solutions that would be reflective of the organization's identity and purpose. A public relations event might still have been part of their plan, but a corresponding struggle with substantive issues would have helped its choice to reflect the heart of the organization, not just be an entertaining event.

I know of no organization that will publicly complain about the Marginal board members, especially if they make significant financial contributions or bring name credibility because of their position and power in the community. If they are "letterhead trustees," they can engender goodwill and public support by association, but if they lack the capacity to care deeply about the organization or lack commitment to the purpose for which an organization exists, there is a diminishment of accountability to the larger community and a chance for erosion of the community's trust. In that case, staff will often want to keep them sealed off for fear of the damage they might do if they were more involved.

Résumé Builders

Individuals who fall into the Résumé Builder category possess an intellectual understanding of altruism, but they lack experience with and understanding of those with whom the organization is primarily in existence to serve, especially if those being served are different in circumstance and background. In spite of their belief that service to others is something good to do, their primary motivation is to do well rather than to do good. They labor in the interest of serving their own career ambitions and in developing more contacts and skills through voluntary service. A major incentive for their board involvement is the development of an impressive dossier that will boost their professional advancement.

Many of these individuals have positional authority and possess a high level of competence and responsibility at an institutional level. They are adept at quickly defining and solving problems and have developed an expertise in having answers rather than in formulating strategic questions. They are identified and valued for specific skills and abilities they can contribute to the organization and are given board responsibilities where these abilities can be used. Individuals in this category have been recognized for their leadership potential and have been mentored and tracked for success in the professional and voluntary sectors. Many have been tapped as the next generation of leaders within their workplaces and communities. In keeping with their anticipated future status and increased institutional authority, they are encouraged to participate in the voluntary sector. Their responses to problems tend to be based on the skills and expertise they bring, which become the lens through which reality is viewed and responses framed.

Often Résumé Builders are asked and agree to serve on multiple boards because of the prevailing mythology that volume of activity and visibility are the equivalent of leadership. The premise is that serving on a number of boards is a demonstration of leadership.

Many companies strongly encourage these kinds of individuals to engage in voluntary activity and contribute to the larger community. It would be a remarkable contribution to the not-for-profit sector if they would also provide and support programs that engage employees in conversations about and preparation for the importance of such service individually, corporately, and communally. Companies could do much to challenge the presumption that competence in the workplace equals competence on boards or in community service. When the assumption goes unchallenged, it limits individual and organizational contributions and their abilities to make the best choices to serve. This assumption perpetuates an attitude of arrogance and leads to practices that reinforce the perception that businesses have much more to teach not-for-profits than not-for-profits have to teach them.

One of the greatest challenges all organizations face, whether for-profit or not-for-profit, is the development of trust and a deep, sustained commitment. An effective way to foster and accomplish both of these is through service in the voluntary sector. Service to the community can help employees better understand the connection between a company's bottom line and larger social issues and needs, to see the interdependence between them and to see preparation for addressing them as a worthwhile investment of a company's resources.

Compassionates

Compassionates are volunteers who are especially knowledgeable about the needs of those whom the organization directly serves—that is, its primary publics. They are committed to the development and effectiveness of programs that the organization offers to meet these needs. These individuals possess a deeply integrated altruism; they care and are passionate about responding to clients' needs. Their service bias is often expressed in a desire to address client needs immediately and to engage in immediate, direct action to alleviate identified problems. This is their major interest: to alleviate presenting problems rather than to identify and prevent the causative factors.

This group includes board members who are knowledgeable about the purpose of the organization and call the organization to be accountable in living out its mission. Their focus of attention and resources tends to be on the immediate and present, a tendency whose consequences can be the diminishment of an organization's ability to attend to and prepare for the long term. These individuals have considerable ability to influence issues, but if they are too focused on addressing immediate needs and tasks, they will find it difficult to distinguish between "doing things right" or "doing the right thing" (Bennis and Nanus, 1985, p. 21).

Individuals in this category often provide much-needed hands-on assistance to not-for-profits, particularly attractive for any organization during economically hard times. Although all types of not-for-profit organizations need these volunteers, their style of operating can be just as shortsighted as that of the Résumé Builders, though it may not be readily perceived as such. Their behavior places the good of the clients and the mission of the organization first. Yet in the long term, this behavior, if it is normative for the group, can put the organization at risk if these board members are unable to put their passion in perspective and see the larger picture. When governance leaders become chiefly concerned about the alleviation of current suffering and press only for immediate responses to client needs, they place the organization's long-term ability to serve effectively in jeopardy.

Although Compassionates' own interests are related to the greater good, client interests sometimes have higher priority than the interests of the organization. Over time this position distorts the lens through which trustees monitor mission and alters their ability to view the relevance and effectiveness of the organization accurately. Organizations where this has happened are frequently puzzled about why their actions are not producing the intended results. If these board members advocate an expanded client base and service delivery system, yet do not see a corresponding need to invest in increasing staff and raising adequate resources, they become party to an overextended organization. When client needs supersede organizational capacity, mission drift can occur. The slippage begins when concern about the immediate needs of one public is allowed to predominate without looking at the impact these might have on an entire system.

Compassionates tend to rubber-stamp decisions as long as client needs are being served. The hazard this group faces is isolation from external realities because there is minimal examination of how the external environment has changed or how the organization has changed. The board's deliberation and decision making are unchallenged as long as the organization can count large numbers of client contacts and have proof of direct hands-on service.

Trustee Leaders

Trustee Leaders combine altruism with authority, acknowledge their self-interest, and balance it with sensitivity to and regard for the common good. They seek to achieve balance between the needs of the individual and those of the organization, and they exercise their responsibilities with genuine care and judiciousness. They are able to see the immediate needs of those being served within the context of broad community needs and the larger world. The responsibility for seeing beyond the organization's present in order to make the best decisions for its future is their concern. Trustee Leaders have learned to express their caring in powerful and empowering ways and to effect change that is substantive, not solely cosmetic. They understand that the health of the organization and the effect on clients' lives depend on a wide and deep view of reality. This view of reality provides a sound basis for deliberation and decision making and helps leaders develop a capacity to create meaning from considerable information as they determine the organization's future direction.

Trustee Leaders exercise their responsibilities out of an ever-deepening understanding of their own individual history and mission, as well as the history and mission of the organization. Their perceptions and judgments are grounded in both inner wisdom and historical experience. These governance leaders demonstrate a knowledge of their personal story, the organization's story, and the multiple collection of individual stories that are expressive of institutional identity.

Trustee Leaders seek to understand personal and organizational mission. They ask the why and how questions of organizations and of themselves: Why does this organization exist? Why does it serve its direct publics? Why does it need to be here in the future? Why do I serve on this board? How are my interests and needs being met on this board? How are my values and beliefs affecting my perceptions and my leadership? How is this organization contributing to the community? How am I contributing to this organization and to the community?

Because they know that a solid understanding of the organization is foundational to their capacity to be effective, they have a depth understanding of organizational history, clarity about its mission, awareness of the context of its service, and an ability to anticipate and project a future into which the organization will move and what will be necessary for it to survive and sustain itself.

These are individuals who value and combine being and doing. They understand the importance of self-examination and self-development as much as they do organizational assessment, environmental scans, and strategic plans. They recognize that they are in a continual process of becoming that affects their ability to serve and that can deepen their capacity to hold an organization in trust. This is the most distinguishing characteristic of Trustee Leaders. These are not perfect people, but they are conscious of their strengths and their limits, and they use this knowledge in exercising leadership and establishing boundaries of service.

Most volunteers have experienced or engaged in some of the behaviors described in all four categories. They shift in and out of these different combinations of altruism and authority in different organizations and at different times; sometimes these shifts can occur within the same organization. It is not useful to label these categories as either good or bad. In fact, the categories can be very useful if they engage boards in reflecting on their composition and on the recruitment, orientation, and education of trustees. This framework of behaviors is a way to help boards discuss their unique and special contribution to an organization.

There are valid reasons that organizations have board members who operate in the Marginal, Résumé Builder, and Compassionate categories; there are desirable attributes in each category, and a diversity of perspectives, skills, and abilities can certainly contribute to an organization's ability to accomplish its mission as well as to see a fuller picture. The chief concern is that if the majority of the board is composed of or dominated by any one of these categories, it would be predictive of serious challenges for the organization. What is important is whether an organization has the vision, capacity, and commitment to invest in the depth education necessary to develop Trustee Leaders. A board that has the intention and a method to make this the normative behavior will develop governance leadership that will foster communities of trust and create not-for-profits of note.

Through sound and comprehensive preparation for their responsibilities, board members can embody both the passion and competencies necessary to attain organizational excellence. The bottom line in the not-for-profit sector and in our communities is not only a monetary one. The bottom line includes the development of capable leadership. This is the factor that ultimately will determine the character, identity, success, and longevity of any organization, especially those the public has entrusted with the responsibility to exercise the gift of service.

Chapter Six

The Power of Giving

To understand trustee leadership fully requires some attention to the practice of giving and the concept of gift, which permeate the expressions of caring and voluntary acts of service in our culture. These are fundamental to depth education and the preparation of volunteers for trustee leadership and involve the cycle of giving and receiving. When this transformative exchange of giving and receiving happens, the gift increases and the circle created expands. Trustee Leaders are aware of their role as "movers of gift" and understand their participation in the powerful tradition of giving embedded in the history and culture of American voluntarism.

The word *gift* conjures up colorful memories and multifaceted meanings. We are reminded of times and moments of remembrance and celebration, or recognition and reward. In every realm of our lives, this word has relevance in our discussion of the philosophy and meaning of voluntary service. Philanthropy examines our motivation for and patterns of giving, and it has provided a comprehensive picture of how we give our money and time. Not studied as extensively is how we are introduced to the tradition of giving and what enables us to sustain our voluntary commitments and giving over time.

The book *Common Fire* is a valuable contribution in this regard (Parks Daloz, Keen, Keen, and Daloz Parks, 1996). The authors interviewed over one hundred people over several years to ascertain what contributed to their ability to sustain long-term commitments on behalf of the common good. One of the questions they explored was what enabled individuals to leave the familiar and engage in a world of global complexity, change, and diversity. The authors discovered that giving was viewed as much more than an exchange of money or a logging in of hours of doing; giving is an expression of powerful cultural and religious values and messages that telegraph identity and development. One such message, "It is better to give than to receive," is familiar and exemplifies the high value we place on giving, and the belief that the giver benefits as much as or more than the recipient of the gift. The mutual benefit derived from giving is one foundational assumption of American philanthropy. This professed preference for giving over receiving is not a statement of superiority over receiving, but rather a reinforcement and affirmation of the obligation of those with resources to give. The capacity to give derives from an obligation to give to those who have less than the giver does.

The capacity to give to those with less is shaped by a belief in abundance (a sense of having more than enough and that having at least enough is possible for everyone), a recognition of the disparity in the distribution of wealth and of the needs resulting from this inequity, and an understanding of being fundamentally in relationship to another. These all combine to create an obligation to act in ways that are both generous and generative. This capacity can be fostered through experience, education, and formation in service and in the traditions and legacies of giving.

Gift through service has developed in different ways in different cultures. For example, in some Native American cultures, the gift is perceived as always moving in a circle, and this continuing movement creates something that transcends both giver and receiver. The circular movement of gift is a powerful force of wholeness and completeness, and it portrays the practice of giving as infinite, communal in nature, interconnected, and ever growing. Lewis Hyde (1983, p. 16) captures this powerful dynamic: "When gift moves in a circle, its motion is beyond the control of the personal ego, and so each bearer must be part of the group and each donation is an act of social faith." The possessor of the gift is naturally expected to share it, and in the sharing of the gift, abundance is created. This process of creation and generativity is central to the notion of gift: the gift increases when it is shared, and it is in the consumption of the gift that it becomes transformative, changing from one state to another. The energy of the gift never dies; it gathers more as it moves, encircling and changing many lives in the process.

A gift acknowledges and represents a relationship—a connected-ness to another. If this connection is realized and giving is perceived as part of something bigger than the act or any one individual (though dependent on the individual for movement and therefore its increase in value), the giver and the receiver discover that they are temporary custodians of the gift. Recipients realize that their ex-pression of gratitude for the gift keeps the gift moving, deepening and widening its impact as the gift is given again. According to Hyde, we "suffer gratitude" between the time a gift comes to us and the time we pass it to others. So giving becomes the true acceptance of the original gift and is passed on as an expression of gratitude. When we truly comprehend what we have been given and experience the grace of gratitude, we have the desire to share.

We can clearly see this cycle and its transformative nature in the practice of potlatch in Northwest Native American tribes. The pot-latch is a significant social ceremonial event commemorating an important occasion in the life of the tribe—for example, a mar-riage, the naming of a child, or the building of a house. The host family affirms its high status through lavish acts of giving to others. In a traditional potlatch, each guest received a gift; the recipient of the potlatch had to give a bigger gift or suffer loss of prestige. The oldest and most universal occasion for this ritual was a transition in tribal leadership. In the potlatch we see not only the associations between abundance and giving, but also the connections between gift and leadership. The accepted leader is the individual who has demonstrated status and is accorded authority through generosity.

Another example of the association between community status and the obligation to share wealth is the Jewish practice of *tzedakah*, a form of giving that expresses the notion that people of different means owe to one another. *Tzedakah* is a Hebrew word meaning both "righteousness" and "charity," and is guided by three princi-ples: help the poor help themselves, treat the poor with respect and dignity, and preserve the anonymity of the donor. *Tzedakah* calls for giving in a spirit of kindness and tenderness while ob-serving the dignity and worth of each individual. At its highest level, the goal is to enable the recipient to become self-supporting. *Tzedakah* is conducted in such a way that respect for the giver and the receiver is manifest in both attitude and action. Giving is done out of a sense of obligation and humility, thoughtfully carried out, and marked by the honor it gives to giver and receiver. Giving becomes a practice perpetuating a tradition that coheres a community through the movement of gift.

In the practices of potlatch and *tzedakah,* the gift is expected to transform, change, or create something better than what existed at the beginning. The expectation that those with greater means give to those with lesser resources is part of the Judeo-Christian religious tradition and has greatly influenced Western philanthropic practices. The Bible is a source of numerous examples of the continual movement of gift and the sense of obligation that it embodies. A number of examples exemplify the philosophy and values that underpin many contemporary practices of giving.

The Book of Isaiah states:

> Is not this the fast that I choose:
> to loose the bonds of wickedness,
> to undo the throngs of the yoke,
> to let the oppressed go free, and to break the yoke?
> Is it not to share your bread with the hungry,
> and bring the homeless poor into your house;
> when you see the naked, to cover him,
> and not to hide yourself from your own flesh?
> Then shall your light break forth like the dawn
> and your healing shall spring up speedily;
> Your righteousness shall go before you,
> the glory of the Lord shall be your rear guard.
> Then you shall call, and the Lord will answer;
> You shall cry, and he will say,
> Here I am. [Isaiah 58:6–9]

This poetic passage, in query form, makes explicit the generosity expected from the giver toward those of lesser circumstances. It is a generosity whose practitioners can be assured will be reciprocated, but not from the recipient and not at a time certain. In these words and the verses that follow, the relationship between the giver's intention and behavior and the effect on the giver's life is addressed:

> The point is this: he who sows sparingly will also reap sparingly, and he who sows bountifully will also reap bountifully. Each one must do as he has made up his mind, not reluctantly or under compulsion, for God loves a cheerful giver. [II Corinthians 9:6–7]

These themes recur in the two following passages from Corinthians and Deuteronomy:

He who supplies seed to the sower and bread for food will supply and multiply your resources and increase the harvest of your righteousness. You will be enriched in every way for great generosity, which through us will produce thanksgiving to God, for the rendering of this service not only supplies the wants of the saints but also overflows in many thanksgivings to God. [II Corinthians 9:10–11]

At the end of every three years you shall bring forth all the tithe of your produce in the same year, and lay it up within your towns; and the Levite, because he has no portion or inheritance with you, and the sojourner, the fatherless, and the widow, who are within your towns, shall come and eat and be filled; that the Lord your God may bless you in all the work of your hands that you do. [Deuteronomy 14:28–29]

These passages express prevalent beliefs and are descriptive of the practices and expectations in which those of a particular tradition are to engage. These eloquent words resonate with the theme of being given to and formed by the act of giving to another. Giving is not portrayed as an act of self-aggrandizement; it is an act of love, respect, and gratitude. And through the expression of these, the cycle of giving generates individual and corporate blessings that keep the generative nature of gift intact.

In the Judeo-Christian tradition, the capacities and practices of giving originate from a belief that the gift is representative of a larger love that inspires and enables individuals to give initially and over time, so that they create and then sustain community. Being loved creates the capacity to love another and becomes the basis for the creation of the capacity to give and to develop community. In this tradition, giving is grounded in the belief that the individual is gifted by, and is therefore an instrument of, this greater love—a love that is generous and generative. The act of giving is an act of love that creates more capacity to give. The knowledge that one is the recipient of a greater love provides the passion and commitment to create opportunities and experiences in which the gift can gather force and momentum. It was this kind of understanding that inspired the contract in which the Puritans made a commitment "to love and serve one another" when they arrived at this continent.

Religious amnesia and sometimes overzealousness about the separation of church and state have dimmed our recognition of the extent that religious beliefs and teachings influence contemporary philanthropic activity and practice. Whether acknowledged or not, they continue to invest deeply in our motivation and practices to care for and serve others; to cross private boundaries and venture out into the public arena; to perceive and respond to chronic, persistent human need; to bring about change in the quality of life for those less fortunate; and to continue to hope and believe that significant differences can be made through giving. The desire to make a difference, to tackle difficult adaptive problems and issues, to solve complex social problems, to improve the quality of life for others, and to transcend the limitations of our individual, private spheres originates from a deep religious wellspring. These are desires that contain the passion and vision of the indigenous and transported peoples of this continent. This is a homeland of persons who did not separate their faith from service or their religious beliefs from their civic engagement. Minimization or denial of these deeply religious and spiritual undercurrents in the practices of giving threatens both our generosity and generativity, and lessens the power to transform the gift and those involved in acts of giving.

D. Susan Wisely, director of evaluation at the Lilly Endowment, has written an enlightening essay describing three traditions of giving: philanthropy as relief, improvement, and social reform. Philanthropy as relief operates on the principle of compassion and seeks to alleviate human suffering; improvement operates on the principle of progress and seeks to maximize human potential; and social reform, of justice. She writes: "Of all the traditions contributing to the contemporary practice of philanthropy, the tradition of benevolence [relief] is most obviously rooted in a religious world view" (Wisely, 1998, p. 8).

Central to all three traditions are a sense of caring for the other and a practice of giving. Though the intentionality of the gift in each tradition may differ, when caring is a part of the cycle, the potential exists for the transformation of both the giver and the receiver.

In the absence of concern or love for one's neighbor, all three traditions risk creating practices that perpetuate the denigration of or power over another individual or group. When these practices are infused with the unique human capacity to see our connectedness and relatedness, giving becomes a recognition of the

dignity and worth of all persons and inspires the continual movement of gift through service and leadership.

The history of the not-for-profit sector chronicles the strong relationships among religion, benevolent societies, and humanitarian
acts. Partnership between the civic and the religious realms of the
community is most apparent in the social reform movement of the
Progressive Era, which was inspired by Christian idealism and heav-
ily influenced by the leadership of women. Religion both informed
the humanitarian spirit of the age and was supported by the political
culture that emerged at the close of the century as the Christian
volunteer and "educated mother" made it possible for the United
States to define and construct the public service sector of an industrial society. Organized church women systematized benevolent im-
pulses and supported the creation of modern urban agencies of
social service. Women brought an ethical and moral dimension to
the political system when they ventured beyond the domestic sphere
to influence public policy in the late nineteenth and early twentieth
centuries. This and other factors made religious values integral to
the political culture of the time (Prelinger, 1992, p. 21).

During the Progressive Era, a resurgence of voluntarism was ac-
tivated by the belief that ordinary citizens who are organized do
influence social reform. Churchwomen from nearly every major denomination actively participated to improve health care, education,
and economic conditions for the disadvantaged. They helped to
start schools, hospitals, and social service programs. It was women
actively involved in their churches who spread the YWCA movement
across the country in order to provide working women with hous-
ing, education, and recreation. The effect of their work can be seen
in the creation of Big Sisters, the Children's Bureau, and the concept of organized voluntary relief for victims of disaster (Ellis and
Noyes, 1990, pp. 170–173).

The organizations created were the harbingers of values and the
manifestation of how these values were to be lived out in community.
They served as the translators and the connectors between the
personal and the private sectors, and they spoke a passionate and
practical language partnered with the practice of behaviors that
considered and shaped the common good.

In his classic essay on Western philanthropic thought, "The
Gospel of Wealth," Andrew Carnegie espoused a strong belief in service for the common good, which he believed was best achieved

through American individualism and capitalism. His belief endured in spite of the inequitable distribution of wealth and the creation of an economic and social caste system. What Carnegie symbolized, and now contributes to our contemporary struggle to reconnect self-interest with the common good, is found in his belief that gifts are to be given for the benefit of the community rather than for the alleviation of individual suffering: "It is a nobler ideal that man should labor, not for himself alone, but in and for a brotherhood of his fellows, and share with them all in common, realizing Swedenborg's idea of heaven, where, as he says, the angels derive their happiness, not from laboring for self, but for each other" (Rockefeller, 1983, p. 100). Further, he is quite prescriptive in defining the standards and expectations of giving for those with substantial means:

> This, then is held to be the duty of the man of wealth; to set an example of modest, unostentatious living, shunning display or extravagance; to provide moderately for the legitimate wants of those dependent upon him; and, after doing, to consider all surplus revenues which come to him simply as trust funds, which he is called upon to administer, and strictly bound as a matter of duty to administer in the manner which, in his judgment, is best calculated to produce the most beneficial results for the community—the man of wealth thus becoming the mere trustee and agent for his poorer brethren, bringing to their service their superior wisdom, experience, and ability to administer, doing for them better than they would or could do for themselves. [p. 104]

Unlike the Jewish practice of *tzedakah*, these words do not convey the deep respect for the equality and dignity of every person in the community, regardless of socioeconomic class. Although they are congruent with the elitist, competitive elements of the potlatch—portraying the wealthy as superior to those of lesser means—they do share the message of responsibility for caring for others and for those beyond one's own self or sphere of self interest. As Carnegie writes:

> The Gospel of Wealth but echoes Christ's words. It calls upon the millionaire to sell all that he hath and give it in the highest and best form to the poor by administering his estate himself for the good of his fellows, before he is called upon to lie down and rest upon the bosom of Mother Earth. So doing, he will approach his end no longer the ignoble hoarder of useless millions; poor, very

poor indeed, in money, but rich, very rich, twenty times a million-
aire still, in the affection, gratitude, and admiration of his fellow-
man, and—sweeter far—soothed and sustained by the still, small
voice within, which, whispering, tells him that, because he has
lived, perhaps one small part of the great world has been bettered
just a little. This much is sure: against such riches as these no bar
will be found at the gates of paradise. [Carnegie, 1983, p. 108]

The ideas of obligation to provide charity to the poor are passionately expressed in these words and express the notion that our
wealth ultimately does not belong to us. Wealth is a trust, and that
trust comes with an obligation to ensure that it becomes a gift that
will continue to circulate and benefit the whole of community.
Carnegie wrote the primer for those who believe the passage, "To
whom much is given much is required."

Whether in the tradition of a Native American potlatch, the Jewish practice of *tzedakah,* or the philanthropic expression of Christian beliefs, we can see the influence of a strong cultural message
that has shaped our philanthropic traditions: giving to others obligates the giver to engage in practices that provide relief from suffering and increase the capacity of others to better themselves and
to improve their circumstances and thereby the circumstances for
the whole of community. When these beliefs are consciously recognized and successfully integrated into organizational structures,
community norms, and individual behavior, community is strengthened and revitalized.

The transforming power of gift results in new ways of being
and doing when it is given out of a recognition of giftedness—out
of an obligation to honor and attend to something larger than ourselves. This kind of giving is not dependent on a quid pro quo; it
comes from an experience of grace, of being and feeling blessed,
of being gifted and special, *not* being better than anyone else. It is
a level of giving that is the ultimate gift, in part sustained by the belief that the reward of being given to is the ability to give. The reward to the giver is to be able to continue the practice of giving.

Practicing this kind of giving requires a kind of vulnerability em-
boldened and sustained only by a faith in something beyond self. It
exacts an attitude to do for others with no expectation of reciprocity. This kind of giving is rooted in a deep sense of being cared for,
in experiences of trust, a sense of abundance, a belief in being a

part of something bigger that transcends the day-to-day work in which we engage. A loss of belief and connectedness to a larger meaning and a larger reality means the foundation for giving can reach no deeper or go no wider than individual self-interest. Where we are able to sustain the practices of nonreciprocal giving, we find ourselves able to participate in those "wider spirits," able to enter gracefully into the gift cycle, draw the masses into community, and receive, contribute toward, and pass along the best of the collective treasures we refer to as culture and tradition. "Only when the increase of gifts moves with the gift may the accumulated wealth of our spirit continue to grow among us, so that each of us may enter and be received by a vitality beyond his or her solitary powers" (Hyde, 1983, p. 39).

Giving solely in order to get is not trusteeship of gift; it is motivated by self-serving beliefs and is an example of individualism run amok. Giving in order to get is an exchange system of credits and debits that reinforces a perception of scarcity; it discourages generosity, creativity, and the sustaining of a cohesive, caring community. The act of giving is not necessarily diminished if the motivation for it is inclusive of self-gain. It is diminished only when self-interest supersedes all other interests, when it lacks the concern for a larger community and does not acknowledge a larger love or faith in a force greater than human beings. When self-interest is seen as an element in the negotiation of the development of community but not given predominant priority over the common good, there is potential for the healthy balance of authority and altruism and therefore for the transformation of individuals, organizations, and the culture. The capacity to engage in this level of giving is deeply connected to spiritual traditions.

The history of giving in the not-for-profit sector is an inevitable encounter with the streams of wisdom from diverse religious and cultural traditions. The ongoing contemporary acts of service in this sector are practices of giving fed by these streams. When we understand our voluntary service as the movement of gift, we can better appreciate the authority we have been given and the impact our service can have on individual formation and organizational and cultural change. We can comprehend the significance of creating and supporting institutions and communities that engage the moral practices of trusteeship. In the practice of sharing ourselves—our time, talents, treasure, and trust—both giver and recipient are nurtured, and community is created and enriched as well. The very thing we help to create nurtures us, and our own nurturance empowers us to continue to give. The gift is moving in a circle.

The facilitation of this movement is one of the characteristics of trustees who are leaders, of leaders who hold in trust. The gift, whatever it is, is not a possession permanently assigned; it is a trust to be held and shared, to be improved on and passed on for the benefit of others. This continual movement of gift between individual and community enriches both.

The not-for-profit sector is one of the few places where we can regularly see the manifestation of the movement of gift: the former client who now serves on the board, the teacher who provides students with the care and attention she received as a student, cancer survivors who start an organization to support those who are struggling to survive, the former recipient of services who donates time and money to the organization's annual campaign, the businessman who establishes an educational foundation for the support of excellence in teaching because a teacher inspired him to high achievement. Each of their stories demonstrates the power of being given to and of wanting to express the felt sense of gratitude in ways that will contribute to a wider sphere of the community and will touch the lives of everyone, including the stranger. In touching the lives of strangers, we reduce the separations and estrangements within ourselves and our communities.

More attention needs to be paid to reclaiming the legacy of trusteeship as gift, of fostering practices of giving. A significant way to begin is through the formation and education of the gift givers: those millions of volunteers who give of themselves daily in the not-for-profit sector, particularly those who govern our institutions.

Part Two

Depth Education for Trustees

Chapter Seven

Preparation for Depth Education

As a country we are at a cross point—one that calls us to remember what is essential from our past and what is useful in making better choices about the future. At a time of rapid economic, sociological, and technological change and increases in the cross-currents of diversity and differences, our capacity to operate from a basis of the common good in addressing problems is being seriously tested. As these changes continue and the complexity of problems grows, our need for the services that not-for-profit institutions uniquely provide will also increase. What kind of institutions will be required? What kind of leadership will be necessary?

"Institutions," says one author, "need two kinds of leaders: those who are inside and carry the active day-to-day roles, and those who stand outside but are intimately concerned, and who, with the benefit of some detachment, oversee the active leaders. These are the trustees" (Greenleaf, 1977, p. 40). Implicit in the use of *oversee* and *detachment* is the need for trustees to see things whole and to take the longer view by benefit of some distance from the daily pressures of the organization's life. The capacity to maintain a wide perspective is essential to a board's ability to lead. Those who serve as trustees of not-for-profit organizations are in significant positions of leadership. Not only are they responsible for developing vision and determining the future direction of the organization, they are also charged with establishing and maintaining the overarching beliefs and values that shape the organization's character, define and guide its work, and significantly affect the lives of those it serves.

Fulfillment of the responsibilities of trusteeship requires both management and leadership abilities. The management role by necessity focuses attention and energy on day-to-day details and tasks, that is, the immediate or intermediate approaches and solutions. The exercise of leadership requires the capacity to retain a view of the whole while remembering the component parts. The larger view focuses trustee responsibility on "doing the right thing, not just doing things right" (Bennis and Nanus, 1985, p. 21), an attribute that distinguishes leadership from management. The shift from a hands-on to a heads-up perspective requires a different conceptualization of service and leadership on a board. We need a nontraditional approach to the preparation, education, and development of trustees who have these capabilities; and whatever form this approach takes, it needs to honor the vocational and covenantal nature of the roles and responsibilities of trusteeship.

Trusteeship is a calling that embraces practices deeply rooted in history and tradition that are worth passing on. The capacity of boards to lead effectively is connected to their ability to recover the sense of vocation and the notion of practices, which when regained can revitalize the not-for-profit sector and provide it and the larger community with leadership necessary for the changing culture in which we live.

These in-between times require a different approach and pedagogy for the education of trustees. Robert Wood Lynn (1984, p. 8), former vice president of religion for Lilly Endowment, explained the need for perceiving and providing the education of trustees in a deeper way: "What happens at the deeper levels, the 'subsoil' of institutional life, is finally more significant than any skill training for a particular position. The strength and vitality of an institution arises from the unseen depths. The best educational programs will help leaders explore the institution's 'subsoil'" (1984, p. 8).

The formation of leaders for the not-for-profit sector needs to be grounded in a historical knowledge of the larger tradition of voluntarism and philanthropy and broadened by the larger societal environment and context within which an organization exists and serves. This is the foundation and perspective from which decisions can be made for the organization and the larger community. The board's perspective and behavior are then framed by the context of the organization's particular history and purpose, its unique core beliefs and values, its map of the external environment and reality, and its reading of the future and vision of its ideal state. Depth education for governance leadership includes all of these elements, each adding a level of exploration and understanding that will help trustees blend prudence with creativity, ensuring growth while maintaining organizational integrity.

An organization's presenting issues and problems do not necessarily define its real issues or needs. They may be symptoms of far deeper problems requiring considerably more work. The organization and any consultant working with it have an important role in clarifying needs, developing a full and shared understanding of what the problem is, and determining the best way to address them. To do this requires an important investment of time and a degree of involvement that may be counter to the culture for most volunteers serving on boards. And although a depth education process would be excellent preparation for leadership, it would be difficult to provide without the risk of creating resistance because it is threatening the status quo. Any assessment of a board's functioning can uncover new or uncomfortable information about the character or culture of the group and the organization. This approach is entirely different from the way most of us have been shaped and formed for our leadership roles in any sector.

It can be relatively easy to succumb to the ethos that boards have people who are too busy and overworked to take time for depth education. The seriousness of the job, however, may dictate taking the time. A story illustrates this point. "A surgeon in a major research and teaching hospital had prepared a group of students who were assisting in performing heart surgery. At a critical point in the operation he looked at them and said, 'You will have only ten seconds to tie off this artery; therefore, take your time'" (Parker Palmer, workshop at Trustee Leadership Development, 1990). Boards are not faced with life-or-death situations like this; nevertheless, over time the pattern and quality of their decision making will affect the health and vitality of an organization. As difficult as the advice is to "take your time," it is wise to have boards that are well prepared for the governance leadership role so that when they face pressing and immediate concerns, they will not succumb to panic or resort to behavior that may jeopardize the organization in the long term. A depth approach to board education asks trustees to be fully conscious of their current actions and their potential effect on future outcomes. A depth education approach to preparation for trusteeship can be a deterrent to quick fixes, impulsive interventions, or responses that go no further than the surface or symptomatology.

Preparing Leaders and Nurturing Trustees (PLANT)™ is a form of depth education that engages governance leaders in a process of preparation and learning from which they can assist an organization in the accomplishment of its mission and position it for sustained excellence and success. The acronym is a suitable description for what occurs in a process of leadership development as the seeds for growing the capacity for trusteeship are planted deeply in or within the cultural soil of organizational life.

The process consists of six elements, each of which is valuable to do alone but which, when done together, maximize the effect of depth education: organizational assessment, a review of the organization's history time line, clarification of its mission, definition of its publics, development of its future, and follow-up to evaluate and assist in the implementation of goals (see Figure 7.1). More will be said about this process in the following chapters, but a brief introduction is provided here.

The *organizational assessment* engages staff and board members in a self-evaluation of the administrative, programmatic, financial, and governance work of the organization. It helps identify strengths and challenges and teaches the board to acquire and interpret information in ways that strengthen its ability to plan responsibly for the future. It involves surveys and interviews with the board, staff, and clients as well as a review and audit of documents and observations. Assessment provides a clearer sense of the organization's internal and external capacity and elicits the issues that need attention.

History is an introduction to the culture and character of the organization. It includes the story of the origins of the organization and the people, events, and issues that have helped shape it.

Mission is a discernment of institutional vocation and an examination of core beliefs and values and their relationship to actions. It is the foundation for evaluating organizational integrity and congruence: Is there a fit between what an organization believes and values and what it does? And mission is the plumb line for decision making: Is the direction an organization has taken an expression of its mission?

Figure 7.1. Preparing Leaders and
Nurturing Trustees (PLANT)™ Process Cycle

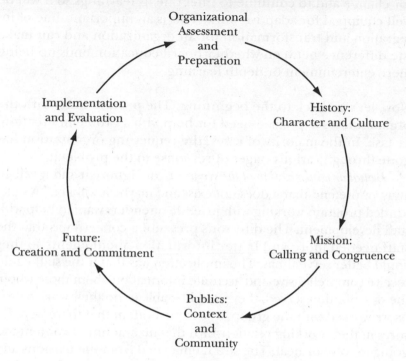

A discussion of *publics* is an opportunity for an organization to see itself in the context of a broader social system. It identifies those who are directly served by an organization and those who are in varying degrees of relationship and connectedness. A discussion of publics aids board members in seeing the bigger picture, in exercising their responsibility for maintaining relationships, in being accountable to the public, and in setting appropriate boundaries of service.

The element of *future* involves envisioning, then translating the vision into a plan of action. This process invites the board to dream a preferred image of the organization's future that is predicated on a solid foundation of knowledge and understanding. The vision must be translated into specific goals, objectives, tasks, and time lines so that the inspirational energies of mission and vision are manifested in reasonable, well-thought-out strategies.

The PLANT cycle then moves into a period of *evaluation and follow-up* that enables the organization to sustain the momentum for change and to continue to integrate its learnings so it will be well equipped for adaptive work. This is an important time of integration and transformation for an organization and can make the difference between whether board education ends up being mere entertainment or depth learning.

Now, let's go back to the beginning. The process starts with the organization's expressed need for help with a problem, situation, or task. In the majority of cases, the requesting organization has gone through various stages of response to the problem:

Denial or minimization of the symptoms, or "Ignore it and it will go away, or pretend that it does not exist and maybe it will not." A state-funded program working with juvenile offenders wanted help with staff development. The director's presenting concern was that the staff needed more and better information about clients so they could better serve them. The implication was that if the staff could receive comprehensive and accurate information about those whom the organization served, they would be able to do their work better. As we worked with the group, it became evident that there were fissures in their working relationships that no amount of content was going to solve or heal. The strain emanated from the tensions and anxieties about racism among the staff within their unit. Even when the information gained from staff interviews revealed this was a significant issue, the staff continued to deny that it was a problem or, if it was, they described it as minor.

Treating the symptoms, or "Address what is visible and immediate." A performing arts center with a history of three directors in five years needed to find yet another new executive director after the board had requested the resignation of the previous one. The board members were exemplary in managing the affairs of the organization during the interim and attended to a number of tasks the executive director had left unfinished. The focus of their concern was on filling the vacant position, not on the board's past processes of selection and oversight.

Postponing the solution, or "There is a problem, but let's deal with it later." The vestry (governing body) of a large suburban church found itself facing a large deficit in the church's budget for the year because of unexpected costs in a capital expansion project. An examination of how this had happened revealed a gross error made in the original proposal. The treasurer had known about the problem but had kept this information from the rest of the vestry. The vestry was forced to address the issue after their newly hired priest had discovered the problem and reported it to the vestry. The vestry members decided that it was best not to confront the treasurer or to share this information with the congregation.

Reframing the problem, or "I thought that the problem was . . . but it's really . . . " Members of this same vestry initially became irritated with the rector's insistence at getting to the bottom of the financial problems but eventually realized that there was a larger issue that needed to be addressed so that the vestry would never again find itself ignorant of the financial commitments made by the church or sign contracts without a more thorough review. Once the conversation shifted from blame and personal attack, the real issues emerged and could be dealt with effectively.

Acceptance and resolution, or "There is a problem, and we need to do something about it." The vestry recognized the need to work on repairing the trust that had been damaged by the absence of accurate and complete data in the hiring process, the need to examine governance, boundaries of accountability, and the negotiation of authority between vestry members and rector.

An organization that asks for assistance is acknowledging that its problems at whatever stage of response cannot be solved using current organizational resources, knowledge, and expertise. But an acknowledgment of these limitations must not be confused with having a clear understanding of the problem. At the point that an organization asks for assistance, there can be considerable ambivalence about getting help; those who work with organizations need to be sensitive to this dilemma and help the organization feel more accepting of help.

Helping an organization clarify what it perceives to be the problem is the most important work an external consultant can do. The organization's initial version of the problem must be received respectfully as their picture of truth. It would be unprofessional, perhaps even unethical, to challenge the veracity of the organization's framing of the problem, but it would be equally irresponsible to assume that the problem as presented is the accurate and complete picture. The most helpful intervention is to provide the organization with many different opportunities to examine its picture of reality. (This is an important function of any assessment.) A good evaluation process will provide several different ways to help an organization view and evaluate itself. It is much like the process photographers use when trying to capture the essence of the object; they take many photos over time from many different angles, using several different lenses, before they capture the right view. It helps an organization see itself in many different ways, in current time and over time.

Chapter Eight

Evaluating the Board's Readiness for Depth Education

Determining an organization's readiness for depth education is a key factor in predicting the success of this approach and the organization's future capacity to apply learnings. One of the most important variables for readiness is the organization's stage of growth and development in the life cycle.

Every organization experiences cycles of growth and development. A board that delegates day-to-day activities to staff and retains responsibility for seeing the big picture and discerning the organizational rhythm and patterns of change will understand these cycles. When governance leaders are aware of internal and external movements, they can anticipate some issues and position the organization to respond to changes effectively.

We have observed four developmental stages that can affect the organization's educational needs and its readiness for learning: creation, institutionalization, community, and re-creation. Each of these stages is linked to the others and affords leaders a chance to explore critical issues and questions affecting the organization's life and that of the community it serves.

Table 8.1 provides a detailed description of critical concerns, key issues, and attitudes in each of the four stages. This information can be useful for engaging board and staff in an assessment of their organization and identifying issues that need their attention. The information in the table can also help to explain organizational behavior and guide the focus of a board's work. In addition, the table

Table 8.1. Stages of Organizational Growth and Development

	Stage 1: Creation	Stage 2: Institution- alization	Stage 3: Community	Stage 4: Re-creation
Organizational concern	What is our identity?	Is this organization viable?	Can we make a differ- ence in people's lives and in society?	Can we change?
Board concern	Can we create a new organization?	How do we want to function?	Are we connected to others, to a larger purpose? What do we want our future to be?	How will we manage change? What changes do we need to respond to? What changes do we need to make?
Key issues	Purpose/mission Membership and development of group to accomplish mission	Establishment of structure, methods, procedures Clarification of roles and responsibilities Development of programs Management of power Concentration on balancing task and maintenance	Developing a culture of trust Congruence between behavior and beliefs Relationships Concentration on maintenance in service of task	Organizational capacity Crisis management Responsiveness Survival

Attitude	Sense of the immediate future Risk High energy Optimism Sense of need	Sense of the immediate future Belief in need for the organization Increased efficiency	Sense of immediate and long-term future Trust Care High energy Commitment	Concern Anxiety Ambiguity
Individual concern	Do I belong?	Do I have influence?	How connected do I want to be?	Will I survive changes?
Skills needed	Leadership Vision Communication Facilitation Knowledge of group development	Organization and administration Team building Conflict management Management of meetings and issues Knowledge of group development Long-range planning	Collaboration Vision Communication Facilitation Knowledge of group development	Adaptability Leadership Vision Ability to consider termination of organization
Common mistakes	Sense of immediacy and no forethought Unclear vision and purpose Failure to lay solid foundation Minimal attention paid to developing trust in the group	Focus on task at the expense of developing the group Inflexible, entrenched leadership Rigidity in structure Crisis management becomes the norm	Too internally focused Loss of touch with publics, external community, and issues No mechanisms in place for renewal of staff and board Resistance to change Denial of death	Failure to revisit organization's history and mission before responding Lack of comprehensive planning Reactionary Shortsightedness

provides suggestions on skills needed for the different stages and identifies common mistakes.

Stage 1: Creation

The beginning phase of an organization's life is a period of gestation of an idea and a concept, and the preparation to make them into something real and tangible. The vision of what can be consumes the founding leader or group and propels them to action. The term *organization* is somewhat misleading because no group exists in much of a structural sense at this point. The architect of the vision and close colleagues who share the vision *are* the organization. They have identified a need and have responded to it in ways that capture the passion of the group and infuse it with motivation and energy. The main emphasis in the creation stage is on responding to an identified need or problem. Even when very experienced professionals are involved, at this stage there is a pervasive sense of the unknown, of new beginnings, of emergence into a disordered place of vast potential that harbors hope and a strong belief that their efforts will make a difference. Fast-paced action and decision making characterize this stage, and the closeness and trust in the founding group helps those involved to manage the high levels of tension and stress that come with bringing something new into the world. If a board does exist, it is likely to be solely for legal necessity, unless it is made up of the founding group or the founder and friends. Primary authority is invested in the visionary leader or the group of leaders who embody the vision—those who are the architects of the mission and direction. As the founding vision takes form, experience and history give it weight. As patterns of consistency emerge, the leadership group recognizes the need, and their responsibility, for a different structure and focus of organizational support if there is to be something lasting. The longevity of what has begun rests with their capacity to bring order and increased commitment to the endeavor.

A neighborhood youth program director asking for assistance in developing a board exemplifies the impact a leader can have at this stage of developing board leadership. The director was unrelenting in pursuing the creation of an activity center that would give the children and youth in her neighborhood a place to go after school and that would provide them with opportunities for learning that could assist them in improving their school performance. Armed with passion and persistence, she persuaded a number of volunteers to work with her. Her energy and optimism were contagious and seemed sufficient to overcome a lack of connections to influential community leaders and a shortage of funds. Even the consultant assigned to work with the group was caught up in the vortex of the vision and donated some of her services. Youth were coming to the program in increasing numbers, and their responses demonstrated a valid need for the services. With the aid of a depth education process, the director and supporters who constituted the board realized that unless they began to look beyond alleviating immediate concerns and just providing safe space for youth, the program would not survive. After this insight, they identified the need for a governance body able to connect this program to a larger community network of support and to begin sorting through the roles and responsibilities necessary to move the program to the next level: institutionalization.

Stage 2: Institutionalization

As the organization seeks to build on the work it began, staff and trustees seek stability. Their work in reorganizing its internal systems of administration, accountability, and communication has a pattern and rhythm. The board recognizes that organizational growth brings with it a new set of responsibilities and a broader and deeper understanding of the needs being addressed. Norms are made explicit and reinforced, procedures and policies are documented, roles and responsibilities are clarified, and boundaries of autonomy and authority established. The trust that existed between a smaller group of people zealous in their devotion to the mission must extend to include a larger group of people, who will not necessarily possess a common history or the depth of passion that existed in the founding group.

Institutionalization is one of the most challenging phases in a young organization's life. The founder recognizes that the creativity and passion that fueled the founding of the organization must now be directed beyond client services and interaction and must also focus on solidifying a service delivery system with the capacity to attend to internal and external demands and needs. A strong desire to expand and share the vision coexists with the awareness that those new to the organization will bring new and different perspectives. The process of educating the new board for their responsibilities and of helping the founder to let go is highly complex—and as complicated as launching a rocket into space. Preparation, sufficient energy, separation, and timing are everything.

A statewide education program for the arts was founded by a dynamic and capable director whose passion for the education of youth created a program that is well regarded for its quality and effectiveness. She began with an idea and built it into an award-winning program and magazine. Everything—program, publications, marketing, fundraising—had her creative, visionary imprint on it, and they reflected her own high standards of quality and excellence. Those in the governance role were from a variety of professional backgrounds, and nearly all shared the founder's passion for educating the public about the arts. As the program grew in stature and impact, the founder and a few members of the board began to realize that they needed to develop a broader base of financial and program support. The board began to be cognizant of its responsibility for the existence of the organization. As the founder reflected on this challenging phase, she said, "I realized that I couldn't be the sole producer of everything if this organization was to grow. It was my baby, but it was time for it to grow up!"

The director, board, and staff went through extensive training over five years to help them develop the infrastructure and governance mentality necessary to lead the organization. Letting go of something that is the personification of the founder is always difficult, and it was for this organization too. The leaders were wise in examining and owning this phase of development. Their recognition allowed them to prepare for and to pace the changes so that the founder could move on and the organization would survive after this separation.

As the organization moves from a state of passionate impermanence to one of structure and stability, there is less dependence on the drive and vision of the leader (or group of leaders) to motivate others to invest in the organization's future. There is as well a growing awareness that there is something worth preserving; it is embodied in the founder yet also independent of this person. Those intimately and those newly involved with the organization see the need for establishing internal systems of support and developing a diverse and ever widening circle of stakeholders. A major challenge for this still new but maturing entity is learning how to retain the vitality of the creative stage through the transition to the new phase of organization and increased accountability.

Division of labor, which was dependent on in-the-moment interest and availability, is now accomplished through job descriptions and roles and responsibilities. Boundaries that were established as the organization encountered new roles are more firmly drawn, although they are subject to reconsideration and renegotiation as the organization's environment changes.

At the same time that the organization must get its internal administrative house in order, it must initiate effective communication and relationships with a wider audience and group of supporters. Marketing and development efforts, which in the past were mostly spontaneous, intuitive, reactive, and staff driven, must now become formally integrated, delegated to particular staff, and shared with the board. The organization widens its view to include not only those it came into existence to serve but other publics as well. When an organization finally believes it will continue to exist in the future, its perspective automatically widens to embrace a broader context and role, and it moves into the stage of community.

Stage 3: Community

In this stage, the organization's capacity to engage in adaptive and integrative work is high, and it is able to retain a high level of congruence between organizational and community perceptions, expectations, and performance. This is a period of internal cohesion and increased connection and accountability to the external environment. The leadership of the organization is a collaborative partnership between staff and board, with appropriate areas of authority invested in the trustees, executive, and program staff to lead and manage the organization. The organization has both a cohesive culture and an administrative stability, and it is able to manage the internal realities while retaining an awareness of the context within which it operates. The increased attention to the external environment is in part necessitated by the need for broader financial support, but it is also due to the organization's understanding of its connection to the bigger community and its role in and responsibility to a larger sphere of society. There is a recognition of the importance of the organization's meaning and contribution beyond the immediate, of determining what legacy it will provide. The leaders understand that the organization exists in relationship with other organizations and has a responsibility for a larger public than just its clients. There is recognition that the organization holds a public trust, which is a reflection of deepened social conscience and moral imagination.

The organization now has a history to draw on. Its past achievements and successes, and its failures and disappointments, have helped to shape its character and identity and provided it with a sense of pride and respect, which leads to a greater confidence and capacity to contribute to the community. A sense of increased security and connection to the community reinforces the organization's care for and investment in the community. When this happens, trusteeship becomes the gift that continues to move in the circle, generating public trust in the process.

The challenges in this stage are complacency and stagnation. The organization needs to be reminded that transition is a normal and necessary part of its life cycle. The management of transition will determine whether the organization can continue to revitalize itself.

Sometimes, even with a consciousness about the need for re-creation and intentional effort to sustain institutional vitality, organizations can find themselves in crisis and decline. They can undergo periods of significant loss in which they are reminded of their vulnerability and the possibility of demise. These may be some of the reasons that organizations can be so resistive to change. Change represents a death of what has been without the assurance of what will be. What is harder to remember at such times is that change is also an offering of new life. Without a "dying" of old views and familiar practices, organizations can become stagnant—itself a form of death. Denial of death as a necessary passage can lead to a state of organizational unconsciousness that can diminish the potential for new growth. To accept death as a phase of change allows room for re-creating the future.

Stage 4: Re-creation

This is the stage of reevaluation, reassessment, and requestioning of ideals and beliefs that the organization holds about itself, its services, and its environment. It can be an important period of rejuvenation. This stage can be anticipated and prepared for, but it is frequently induced by a crisis rather than a conscious, intentional effort to return to a stage of chaos, which is what this stage feels like to those who think that coming to maturity means permanent order. The same sense of chaos that existed in the beginning stage of an organization's development can arise now, but because the organization has an established identity and history, more is at stake and the chaos is perceived as higher risk and far more threatening.

Choosing to change is the adaptive challenge confronting the organization. It must decide what changes are needed, how best to make them, in what order of priority, and at what pace. Those responsible for the organization experience a heightened sense of risk and opportunity; they understand the need to be decisive yet prudent in their choices. Which values will prevail and continue to shape the organization and its programs is a key question, whose answer will determine how well the organization can function in the future. The shape of its future is linked to how well it can assess its past and current capacity, how open it is to the possibility of death, and how capable it is of returning to the creative center from which the sparks of the original mission and founding passion can be reignited so that governance and program leaders can rekindle their commitment and reinvest in strengthening the organization.

An East Coast firm specializing in conflict management and successful by every measure—competent staff, profitability, client satisfaction, superb products, name recognition—found itself at a cross point. It could declare success, bask in its achievements, and continue doing what had gotten it to this point—or it could step back to see what and how it might do things better. The partners realized the risks of reexamining the organization's success and knew that staff anxiety would likely rise, so they sought consultation in managing the process. They examined their culture and historical gestalt, and assessed what advantages and limitations existed in continuing as they had been or in changing their services and target clients. The organization's history held the seeds of the future: it not only regrounded staff in the organization's passionate beginnings and core values but freed people to imagine new and creative ways of structuring the organization and its current and future work. The depth education process produced an invigorating restatement of mission and reinforced a collective agreement that a name change was now appropriate. There is now a stronger sense of allegiance to key principles and values and a new and dynamic visual representation of how their "new" identity, mission, and services will be expressed.

No one model or chart can suffice in describing the stages of an organization's life, nor can it serve as the final arbiter of an organization's readiness, but it can be used as a way to enter into deep discussion of issues that matter in an organization's life as it begins to develop and practice trustee leadership. The process explained in the following chapters reflects the experience of working with hundreds of organizations and leaders, and it is offered as a method of inviting and stimulating ongoing discussion that can lead to improved understanding of an organization and clarity about what the focus and content of its education needs to be.

Chapter Nine

Organizational Assessment

In addition to being cognizant of an organization's stage of development, it helps to have an assessment of where it is in its cycle of work. There are certain key questions in this regard that can be asked in order to determine whether this is the appropriate time to introduce a depth education process:

- What is the organization's annual cycle of work? (Define known projects and major tasks.)
- Where is the organization now in accomplishing these projects and tasks?
- What major deadlines are looming (for example, the final budget is due to the United Way, a proposal is due to a funder, or an audit is scheduled)?
- Is there a major staff change or financial crisis in process (for example, is the board getting ready to fire the executive director, increase or decrease staff positions, or change the executive director's responsibilities)?
- What has been the board's history of trustee education, and how has it responded?
- How would you describe the organization's current interest in, motivation for, and commitment to board education?
- What resources is the organization committing to support this work?
- Are the resources adequate to achieve the goals?

Answers to such questions can help an organization decide whether it is timely and prudent to proceed with this kind of educational endeavor, and what should be the focus and format of the board's work. (Also see Resource D.)

Assessment presents an opportunity for the board to read reality truthfully and determine how the organization can respond responsibly. It provides another way to develop a common understanding from which an organization's energies and talents can be mobilized for problem solving. Also, it enables the organization to decide whether it is prescribing appropriate responses to situations and helps it to determine the best time to engage in educating the board. Although a process of depth education of trustees can be helpful to a variety of organizations, with problems ranging from mild to severe, the considerable commitment of time necessary for depth education means that it is optimally done when the organization is not distracted or consumed by major financial, personnel, or programmatic crises. In crisis the immediate and most pressing needs must be attended to first; their origins can be ascertained and addressed later.

Following are some of the primary indicators as to whether an educational approach such as this will be useful to an organization in need of assistance:

- A demonstrated capacity for learning
- An ability to undergo critical examination and reflection
- A commitment to give the time required
- Compatibility with the philosophy of trusteeship
- A commitment to continuing education of the board and organization beyond the formal educational experience

Boards are encouraged to have a conversation about each indicator, which helps them to arrive at a good decision and launches them into a process of self-assessment and evaluation of their capacity for immediate and sustained education. The criteria move a board from the arena of technical responsibilities into the arena of adaptive leadership. The shift is a signal to a board that scheduling an educational retreat may be as simple as setting a date, but the planning and expected outcomes for it require a complex set of skills if the goal is to accomplish tasks successfully and develop the board into a capable group of governance leaders. This kind of preparation for leadership education and trusteeship will require adequate time, and a retreat is recommended. The retreat may last from one and a half to two days, preceded by several days of planning and several days of follow-up and annual evaluation sessions. The actual time necessary would be determined by the objectives of the retreat.

An organizational assessment process can also be helpful in identifying whether the roles and relationships between trustees and staff are clear, constructive, understood, and responsibly practiced and whether the structure of relationships and functions is appropriate and effective. When there are problems in these areas, it is essential that they be acknowledged and a determination made about their effect on the organization before proceeding with board education. For example, an organization that is feeling muddled about its mission or is in a skirmish over roles and relationships will need additional assistance in order to receive benefit from a process of depth education.

Providing specific information and education to an organization about board and staff roles may need to be the first intervention, but it need not be the only information provided. Where there is ignorance or confusion about role, there is likely to be misinterpretation of a board's leadership responsibilities and understanding of trusteeship. There is a wealth of resources addressing the roles and responsibilities of a board and staff, and many are useful in helping the board to deal with practical issues like developing by-laws, scheduling meetings, structuring and assigning committees, and creating job descriptions.

More resources are needed to help boards manage the adaptive work—for example, defining and mediating the role and responsibilities of the board and executive staff; recruiting and educating board members; monitoring the mission; developing public support; and clarifying issues of authority, accountability, and autonomy. The edict that "boards set policy and staff carry out policy" sounds simple and clear, but it is open to many interpretations. A shared meaning will come from involving board members in a discussion of what it means in general and then more specifically how it will be applied in their organization. Guidelines for board effectiveness always need to be reinterpreted and renegotiated for each board. Imposing any prescription for excellence in governance, including one in this book, is not helpful to any organization. Each organization's culture and context need to be considered in the application of a model of governance. Institutional practices, fundamental assumptions, and operating beliefs affect the ways in which models are understood and the ways in which they can be applied within the organization. What works now may not work at another phase in the organization's life cycle, so the vigilance of the governance leaders will help them to detect when organizational behavior is outmoded or when there is slippage between what is in print and what is in practice. The renegotiation and reinterpretation of relationships and responsibilities, and the matching of educational processes with the distinctive character and needs of a board, is one of the most important capacities in the governance leadership.

External consultation can provide assistance in clarifying the roles and relationships of a highly functioning board, but it is the ability of the board to negotiate these issues that can make the difference between whether it operates smoothly or becomes ensnared in power struggles. Such discussion can be the foundation for reaching agreed-on standards of what an effective board looks like for this particular organization and of coming to clarity about and making a commitment to the changes.

I have worked with numerous organizations whose deeper understanding of trusteeship evolved after an experience of depth education. Only after going through the process did the board and staff see a need to redefine and restructure their relationships and their work. In other instances, the work on clarifying and negotiating roles and responsibilities must come first because the crossing of boundaries is interfering with the functioning of the organization and the ability of people to work together.

If information received from this kind of assessment indicates that depth education is not appropriate or the time is not right, then the organization can be given an explanation as to why this is so. When feedback is given in a way that is respectful of the strengths of the organization, it can be a valuable way for an organization to prepare itself for depth education at a more opportune time. An explanation is useful with any educational process being considered by a board. Saying no to this process need not be a permanent decision, and understanding what would make this level of board education a better fit is valuable information to have.

Once the decision about participation is made, a more formal and substantive organizational assessment process can begin, which will increase the organization's knowledge and understanding.

Assessing an Organization

If we return to the workshop activity in which virtual strangers are asked to plan each other's lives, we are reminded of what a dangerous limitation ignorance of the person can be, and how ignorance can contribute to a distortion of reality. A significant responsibility of trusteeship is the work of collecting accurate and thorough information and knowledge about the organization. Commitment to board leadership involves a great deal more than an acquaintance with staff titles, mission statement, by-laws, and institutional name. One valuable contribution that trustees make is their ability to gather comprehensive data that reveal knowledge about the organization's identity, character, culture, and capacity. This begins with organizational assessment—the trustees' reading of internal reality. The organization is helped to gather comprehensive data about itself and to examine and evaluate this material in order to make the best decision about participating in board education, especially when it is a depth education process that closely involves the board in preparing for its learning and leadership. The assessment uses a set of questions that has been adapted and developed in consultation with representatives of the board and designed to clarify the needs and concerns of the board. The board analyzes the responses to the questionnaire in order to determine whether to pursue this process and, if so, how it can be best tailored to its unique issues and concerns. The design of an educational experience that addresses the specific issues of the organization is developed in consultation with the organization's board and staff. The assessment process, from beginning to end, is owned by both those who govern and those who administer the organization. The assessment will provide the organization with a first reading of its major issues and concerns and its readiness to address them.

A comprehensive assessment of the organization will include conversation with and information gathering from a variety of constituents with different views and experiences. This process brings the organization into partnership with the professional working with it to clarify organizational issues, specify the organization's needs, and evaluate its capacity to engage in learning and its ability to enter into and undergo the process of change. During the assessment phase, board members have opportunities to use their skills of analysis, interpretation, and meaning making—all central responsibilities of trustees.

A center for the development of clergy leadership called for help in dealing with a conflict between the board and the director over a personnel matter. The organization had not engaged in a thorough self-assessment for some time, even though it had completed several strategic plans. The board president wanted the board to develop another such plan. The board and staff understood the need for a retreat but did not quite see the importance of conducting an organizational assessment. They consented, but only reluctantly. The assessment identified a general understanding of, but not consensus on, the organization's mission. A number of members were concerned about its current relevance and were conflicted about what were the priority served groups. In addition, the assessment revealed serious confusion and anxiety about the relationship with the organization's host agency and a pattern of incomplete data possessed by both the new and more veteran board members.

The organizational assessment process is tantamount to holding up a mirror to the organization to help it see itself fully and clearly. In this case, an unobstructed view provided an honest picture of what the organization needed to address in order to reach its goals and improve its position. When the group was given feedback from the assessment and the recommendations for next steps, they realized the urgency of the matter without being overwhelmed with anxiety. Defensiveness about the need for depth education dissipated.

The organizational assessment results and the process of looking in the mirror can be a shock to an organization that has not spent much or any time looking back or reflecting on the past and the lessons and meaning it offers. The impact of hearing feedback can be powerful, so it needs to be done in a way that opens up conversation and enables adaptive change. This should be done by the consultant rather than a board or staff member so that the data is heard with a minimum of board baggage. In the case of the clergy leadership center, the retreat was very productive because the board could address the factors that had enabled and hindered its growth with a collective wisdom and insight gained from the assessment rather than reacting solely to the limited perspectives of personal recollection and interpretation.

Organizational assessment is an antidote to generating solutions detached from the real problems. Problems can be better identified and solved when they are not camouflaged under layers of symptomatology, and assessment in depth education moves beneath the symptoms. When problem definition is clear, the quality of problem solving automatically improves. Organizations that take the assessment process seriously will be positioned to respond to issues more responsibly. The sudden demise of an organization is not likely to stem from not conducting a proper assessment, but its capacity to carry out its mission with care and competence will be compromised in the long run.

Assessment can give voice to all parties and provides an important way to equalize the hearing and emphasis given to the data. On boards or in organizations where significant power differentials exist or a subgroup dominates the agenda and the conversation, the assessment can help to provide opportunities for everyone to be included and to have their thoughts and opinions respectfully considered.

One organization in which the communication had broken down, to the point of personal attack and scapegoating of members, found it nearly impossible to engage in a group conversation without letting the talk degenerate into word exchanges that in no way helped them to arrive at an understanding of the real issues. Group members in meetings would find it difficult to listen to one another or to suspend judgment long enough to listen to what was being said, and they would leave meetings with a garbled and distorted version of the events, which escalated the conflict while blurring the causes of the problems even more. Splinter groups formed, and divisions of old guard and new guard surfaced. The assessment process served as an important way for many different opinions and perceptions to be fully expressed, and it permitted someone with a much greater sense of objectivity and detachment to sift through the information and identify key issues for group consideration and evaluation. Conducting an assessment with this organization served as a boundary-setting function for the work of the group, lowered the very high levels of anxiety, and helped to stop some of the negative acting out of some members.

A process of assessment that is internalized within a culture and is made a part of its practice and ritual can be especially effective. When it is not an integral part of the culture, it is more challenging to use it in the constructive ways described; nevertheless, making it a conscious and formal process can be useful. Optimally, an assessment can be scheduled once a year; minimally, every three years. In a time between times, when change itself is changing, stepping out of the press of the moment in order to gain a more accurate reading of reality and a more realistic perspective of an organization and its context is essential to survival.

Assessment is so important in any educational process or significant organizational change that resistance to it can be puzzling. But if we explore the resistance, we find that there are several reasons for it. One of the most frequently cited reasons is the amount of time it takes. It is time-consuming, and because the results are not as tangible or immediate as having a strategic plan or raising a certain amount of dollars, some find it hard to justify setting aside the time. Other reasons, perhaps less conscious, are the high level of comfort and familiarity that members in an organization have with predictable routines and unquestioned assumptions they have about themselves. In a few instances, the lack of assessment may be the result of the belief that not-for-profits should not be held to the same standards as for-profit businesses when it comes to evaluation. Perhaps the greatest obstacle to engaging an organization or board in an assessment process is that it increases vulnerability and requires an openness to learning something new. Acknowledging or risking more public exposure to weaknesses or inadequacies is uncomfortable, yet this is the behavior of real learning and transformation.

Assessment may be costly, and it is hard to obtain funds for organizational evaluation in a culture that values immediate tangible results. High expectations for organizational evaluation can coexist with inadequate resources for thorough and substantive evaluation. Monetary assistance to organizations seeking to engage in a thoughtful process of self-reflection and learning that can provide reliable information for planning the future is a valuable gift with a high return. Such support can generate an enormous cycle of creative development and change. We may criticize organizations for their lack of substantive planning, but if this is to change, support must be provided for the practices needed for success, and organizational assessment is one of them.

Request for Assistance: The First Step

The process of working with an organization most often begins with a request for assistance. The response is an inquiry for clarification and understanding. The facts as initially presented may not be in dispute, but neither are they accepted as the full and absolute truth. The first attempt at understanding the presenting problem is a first reading; there will be more readings before the full story is known. The attitude of both the consultant and the organization needs to be one of openness, exploration, and partnership in which there is mutual learning. What is most helpful at this point are the capacities to create trust; to listen for spoken and unspoken communication (which I call listening with a "third ear"); and to gather and interpret information. Once the request is understood, the consultant can better determine whether a continued relationship is best or if referral to another resource is more appropriate.

Once the need for and interest in exploring depth education for a board is established, meetings are scheduled with the organization's executive director, selected staff, and the full board or board representatives. The agenda of these meetings is to define the organization's issues and needs, facilitate a conversation about the elements of depth education, and articulate the organization's and board's responsibilities for participating in this process. If there is agreement to continue to proceed, then the organization is given assistance in selecting a group of six to eight trustees and staff to form a resource committee (see Resource F). The committee assists in the collection and compilation of assessment information and prepares the resource material needed for the board retreat. This committee will research the documented history and the observed history, and prepare the organization's history time line. It also organizes, manages, and conducts interviews with former trustees, staff, clients, funders, community leaders, and the community at large.

The decisions about what information needs to be collected are just as important as the activities of analyzing and interpreting. The right data need to be collected in a comprehensive way that ensures confidentiality for those surveyed or interviewed. Both the adaptation and administration of the survey instruments and interview questions are important steps in obtaining ownership of board and staff for their own education over the long term.

An assessment of the organization from the multiple perspectives of executive director, board, key staff, and volunteers is used in planning the board's educational experience. Information obtained from interviews and surveys is augmented with agency records and documents; direct observation of staff, trustees, clients, and other volunteers; attendance at meetings and events; and observation and review of programs. Board minutes; by-laws; profiles of board members; previous consultation, training, and planning processes; and the results of these experiences are also very useful. The more that is known about the organization, the better able the board and executive staff will be to make prudent choices for the organization and their own development. This intensive self-scrutiny and reflection is a valuable way to prepare and position the board to engage in ongoing learning and assume the responsibilities of holding the organization in trust. This approach helps board members gain a broader perspective and deeper comprehension of the organization, and it better prepares them to be entrusted with the governance and leadership role they assume as trustees.

Preparation for depth education positions a board for reflection and discussion of the organization's history, mission, publics, and future. These four elements form the experiential core of the depth education experience. In this process, organizations can be helped to transform themselves and those who serve them. This process of transformation and leadership formation is deeply rooted in trusteeship. Through an educational process like this, trustees and organizations can be helped to build their capacity to lead and to understand their special role as trust holders.

Chapter Ten

Recovering the History That Shapes Us

Many requests for assistance come from not-for-profits at a time when there is an immediate need or problem to be addressed, and the last thing the organization is poised to do is look back in time at the origins of the presenting issues and problems. They want answers now. Typically they are unaware that the seeds of the appropriate solutions are likely to be embedded in the organization's past. Dealing with issues as if they have existence only in current time can lead to a distorted version of what the presenting problem or need is, with little understanding of how the problem came into existence.

Historical reflection helps a board achieve a comprehensive and balanced view of an organization. The organization's time line contains information about what really happened and factors that created significant events, how people responded, and the impact of their responses. There is considerable unpacking of data necessary to understanding organizations and the events that change its life. Carl Dudley, professor at McCormick's Theological Seminary, reminds us that an organization can change its program (what people do) but not the process (how people do things), and when this is the case, things will keep going on as they had been; or the organization can change the process without changing the program and people have changed but not know it (1990, p. 3). A depth approach to education helps organizational leaders change *how* they do things, not just *what* they do.

In Western culture there is considerable ambivalence or resistance to seeing the relevance of the past to the present or to the future, and we generally do not believe that significant change can come from looking back rather than forward. Typical responses initially from board members to a retrospective, reflective approach range from polite tentativeness to strong opposition: "Don't you think what's going on now is more important than what happened before?" "We can't change what happened, but we can affect what happens in the future." "It doesn't matter what happened back then!" "Let the past be the past." "Our problem is the past. Why return to it?" "We have to be forward thinking." "The future needs to be our concern. We have to look ahead!" These responses sometimes are paradoxical combinations of certainty and doubt—a series of words bracketed by both exclamations and question marks, as though waiting for reassurance of their rightness. Nevertheless, the connection between the past and present is bridged not by dualistic thinking but through the holding of both the past and the present together. Bob Lynn, former senior vice president for religion at the Lilly Endowment, Inc., and an independent scholar, reminds us how important it is to embrace both in this memorable observation: "An institution whose leaders are out of touch with its movement through time—its trajectory—is often in serious difficulty. Historical amnesia is always debilitating and occasionally fatal" (1984, p. 8).

The process of engaging in a historical review and analysis of an organization does take the viewer back in time, and looking back can be perceived as a regressive act, a waste of time, a reversal of progress, or justification for keeping the status quo. The truth is that there is potential for the misuse of history as expressed in all the ways we fear, but its potential to release energy and creativity in organizations and leaders is far greater than the risk of regression or stagnation. Organizations need to be introduced to their history in ways that are invigorating and liberating. A depth approach to the education of board leadership enables this to happen.

Developing the capacity to hold an organization in trust acknowledges that history is both a point of entry to and a portrait of the culture; it can be accessed through three basic sources: observation, documentation, and memory. All three of these sources of history are valid and together offer a comprehensive view of organizational history.

Observation—through looking at the physical facilities, attending meetings and programs, watching the interactions of and between staff clients and board members, and seeing the services that are provided—is an opportunity to see how history is manifested in organizational behavior, norms, mission, and practices.

Documentation is a more familiar source of historical information obtained from an organization's written records—for example, board minutes, annual reports, newsletters, articles, brochures, and photographs. These frequently represent the public face of the organization: how it perceives itself and wants to be thought of and remembered. Paper or computer stored files can be chronicles of dramatic and subtle changes over time whose import can be known only in retrospect.

The third source of history, memory, relies on human storage of information and the ability to recall it with reasonable veracity. It calls forth what people who were and are in the organization remember about it from its inception to the present and taps into the rich oral tradition of the organization. Remembered history is a collection of the many public and private stories told about the organization by staff and board members past and present.

When the Mary Reynolds Babcock Foundation board needed to replace its executive director, the members instinctively drew on their collective wisdom to find a leader whose capabilities matched their vision of the future and anticipated changes. They selected Gayle Williams, an experienced educator, administrator, and former senior program officer at the Lilly Endowment to help lead them into this future. Williams's knowledge of depth education and affinity with the concepts of trusteeship, in combination with several board members who shared her understanding of philanthropy as a public trust, launched a process of education that has catalyzed a recommitment to the foundation's core values and a vision of social justice and reform. During the hiring process, Williams and the foundation board explored questions related to the responsibilities of a foundation as a public trust, and several board members who embodied these beliefs served an important role in educating and translating these concepts of trusteeship to the larger board.

Their deep convictions about the philanthropic tradition at the Mary Reynolds Babcock Foundation contributed to a deep knowing that guided the board in selecting an appropriate leader for the time. Immediately on assuming her duties as executive director, Williams interviewed all board members in order to find out their hopes, aspirations, anxieties, and concerns. Some of the questions asked of them were, What are you most proud of? What has been most rewarding? What do you want the foundation to be in ten years? (At the time it was the year of their fiftieth anniversary.) What is most frustrating? What do you want to be different? She then put together a memo that incorporated their vision of what they had said and offered them several options for achieving the vision. The board assumed a posture of listening, organizing, and orchestrating the work that would be necessary to accomplish what was envisioned. They decided that they would need to suspend new grant-making initiatives for a year in order do this. This was a time in which the board achieved a clarity of knowledge and understanding about the character of the foundation and developed its internal capacity for self-reflection and managing change. The board increased its sense of pride in the history and heritage of the foundation, which it now holds in trust and is passing its legacy on in the vision for the future.

The executive director's perceptive reading of the foundation board and its own accurate reading of larger issues and realities contributed to the development of an educational experience rooted in the character of the institution while also placing it in the context of a larger philanthropic tradition. This assessment helped the board to challenge its fundamental assumptions and decide which values and practice to retain. The foundation's historic legacy of trusteeship, the willingness of leadership to risk probing the depths of its culture, and the shared sense of a need to prepare for change were key variables in this process of depth education.

Although Williams's notable skills as a consultant and educator were useful early in the process, she felt that it was essential to have outside consultants to guide this process from design to implementation. These consultants were trusted professionals whose readings were sometimes different from those that Williams and the board had. These outsiders' perspectives proved to be immensely valuable, and when paired with insiders who had what Williams describes as "a genetic code for trusteeship," the board was able to engage in the adaptive work of redefining and repositioning itself to carry out the foundation's purpose effectively.

Central to this process of board education was the goal of creating a program centered in the core values of the foundation. To ensure clarity, meaningful dialogue, and consensus, the group met over a six-month period and conversed about fundamental assumptions. They identified their understanding of human nature and social change, clarified their philosophical basis for social action, and explored the broader traditions of philanthropic thought as a context for examining the Babcock Foundation's tradition. A historical context infused the process: they returned to the institution's founding vision and formative moments and wove together the recorded, remembered, and observed history using legal and program documents, interviews, and an evening of rich remembering and storytelling.

The board also read and studied social theory and social change and researched issues facing the foundation's geographic catchment area. This year-long inquiry both better informed the board and reinforced the role of the board as trust holder. It also instilled a depth process and discipline that better prepared them for their responsibilities as policy setters and reinforced the board's responsibility to exercise broad oversight. As a result, the foundation's governance and administrative leaders were able to articulate clearly the mission and vision and could then initiate and host a series of productive conversations with a variety of its publics in a larger sphere of the community.

The conversations and site visits in which the board participated helped them develop their capacity to "read reality responsibly"—to see the current issues facing their organization and to anticipate future trends—and helped them shape specific strategies that were cognizant of client needs, consistent with the foundation's core values, and considerate of its resources. The foundation came to see even more clearly its role in supporting efforts to rid communities of the debilitating existence of racial and class tensions, which they perceived as major deterrents to strong, healthy communities.

The touchstones for decision making were the core values and operating principles. The board identified three themes, which continue to guide the foundation's work:

- Ensuring the well-being of children, youth, and families
- Bridging the fault lines of race and class in our society
- Investing in human and natural resources for the long term

The foundation decided to invest in the organizational development of grassroots organizations and statewide and regional not-for-profits that support them. It intends to help these organizations develop their capacity to fulfill their mission and sustain their work. It also has the goals of nurturing new approaches to community problem solving, civic engagement, and public dialogue and of helping to establish and sustain collaborative partnerships and networks that are needed to build just and caring communities. The fostering of the capacity of grassroots leaders and the investment in social entrepreneurs and change agents to tackle the toughest community problems reflect the deep trust the foundation has in those it serves and its belief that their effective involvement is essential to meaningful long-term solutions.

The priorities for funding are congruent with the foundation's reading of context, its core values and guiding principles, and its sense of its own historical identity and tradition. In addition, the foundation positioned itself to respond to emerging possibilities in the future and is prepared to make small, nonrenewable grants to organizations whose values and efforts are consistent with those of the Mary Reynolds Babcock Foundation. The application process for potential grantees launches their organizations into a similar process of reflection on their own mission, purpose, and core values.

The Babcock Foundation took a bold step in redefining its role as a foundation and demonstrated the transformative nature of a process of depth education for trustees and staff inclusive of the elements of history, mission, publics, and future. The effect has been a reclaiming of institutional identity and character and an ability to act with an even clearer sense of authenticity and integrity. Although few not-for-profits can afford to give their trustees a year-long sabbatical or suspend new activities for a year, there is much nevertheless that can be adapted from the process and applied to not-for-profit boards.

The responsibility of holding an organization in trust begins with a depth understanding of the organization—an embracing of history in all of its complexity. Holding in trust means having a knowledge of the lived history of an organization—the story and significance of its life over time. Such historical insight and reflection are foundational to effective trusteeship. A review of history immerses trustees in the organization's life over time so that a fuller identity of the organization and the meaning of its past can be discerned. The journey through the past is an intricate weaving of individual stories and corporate story, connecting the individual with the organization and the organization with the environment. It is a bringing together of the little stories with the big story, private memories with public images, in ways that are restorative of the passion and commitment an organization needs from leadership. A historical time line and the exercise of reflection and analysis tell leaders how the organization came into being, how it has been sustained, and the role that key individuals and events have played in its life over time. Perhaps more important, the hearing of collective stories reminds all of those in positions of organizational leadership of their connection to its purpose, the value of their involvement, the need for their service, and the import of their shared contributions to something greater than any one individual or interest.

The Power of Story

We are deeply influenced by stories. Most of us have grown up with fairy tales, myths, and fables that helped to shape our understanding of our selves, of others and the world, and of our relationship to them. Story performs several functions: it tells us important things about others—what is important to them and how they have responded to joy, disaster, success, defeat. It is a window to the soul, a view into the character of an organization. It enables us to see and manage our own internal issues and conflicts; it mirrors ongoing and universal dramas in significant realms of our lives that we do not always have direct access to, allowing us to hear with some distance and to have a fuller comprehension of our lives. Story gives us ways to find meaning in life and muster the courage to solve problems.

Those who grew up hearing fairy tales understand that the power of stories resides in the fact that they are about the inner realm and workings of life. The fairy tale contributes to the development of a mature consciousness that helps civilize the chaotic forces of the unconscious. The role of history is quite similar. History is a portrait of organizational character and culture revealed through story; understanding the story can evoke valuable information that can be difficult to obtain directly and without which it is difficult to help an organization change. The collective stories accumulated over time form the lore of the organization and powerfully form and inform its trustees and staff.

Sharing history through stories helps us to obtain information we cannot have direct access to and provides insight into the inner life and the deeper levels of an organization. History is a powerful way for board members to apprehend the essence of the organization for which they have assumed significant responsibility. The sharing of individual and organizational story builds community and connects individuals to fundamental assumptions, which shape the organization's view of itself and of reality. History is a carrier of significant lessons and messages, a reflector of values and beliefs, the provider of inspiration and hope, insight, and meaning.

The history of an organization is a unique story. More than a chronicle of facts, it is a manifestation of institutional memory: a combination of recorded and observed experiences, significant people, events, issues, problems, and successes that have shaped the organization over time. It is the framework for depth education and helps a board and staff to comprehend the culture, character, and identity of the organization through capturing its movement through time. When all three of the elements of history are connected, a richness of understanding develops and becomes part of the reservoir of wisdom the organization can use in its decision-making and planning responsibilities.

Every organization, no matter what its stage of development, has a story. Like most individuals who are asked to reveal their identity publicly, organizations provide the artifactual and organizational data that are commonly known and help to maintain a positive public persona. Certainly the desire to project the best image possible is appropriate, but the trustees of an organization are also responsible for knowing the full story and for keeping what is publicly known congruent with internal values so that the organization operates ethically and with integrity. When trustees are willing to explore the deeper, more private levels of institutional life, where the seeds of both rebirth and demise reside, they can ensure a higher level of integrity and congruence. Trustees often enter a culture that at the deepest levels is foreign to them and that they will come to know over time if they are fortunate.

Reading Organizational Culture

Understanding culture is never an easy task, in part because it cannot be directly apprehended or comprehended. According to Edgar Schein, author of *Organizational Culture and Leadership,*

The term is frequently misdefined and should be reserved for the deeper level of basic assumptions and beliefs that are shared by members of an organization, that operate unconsciously, and that define in a basic "taken-for-granted" fashion an organization's view of itself and its environment. These assumptions and beliefs are learned responses to a group's problems of survival in its external environment and its problems of internal integration. They come to be taken for granted because they solve those problems repeatedly and reliably. This deeper level of assumptions is to be distinguished from the "artifacts" and "values" that are manifestations or surface levels of the culture but not the essence of the culture. [1990, p. 7]

Organizational history reveals culture. Always a mixture of myth and fact, of realism and idealism, of stability and chaos, it reveals a shared understanding of a particular group about what was and is and identifies its particular rites of recognizing and responding to change and transition. Schein (1990, p. 8) writes that "culture should be viewed as a property of an independently defined stable social unit. That is, if one can demonstrate that a given set of people have shared a significant number of important experiences in the process of solving external and internal problems, one can assume that such common experiences have led them, over time, to a shared view of the world around them and their place in it. Culture, in this sense, is a learned product of group experience and is, therefore, to be found only where there is a definable group with a significant history." History is revelatory of culture and can be a powerful way to access the multiple layers of institutional life.

The historical reflection by trustees is a revisiting of the organization's significant transitions and the mythology associated with and developed from them. The similarities between the phases of organizational life and what Campbell called the "hero's journey" ([1949] 1969, p. 30), or the "monomyth," are striking. The journey or transition involves a separation from what is familiar, movement into the unknown (chaos), and a reemergence during which the learnings experienced during the process are integrated. The transition or journey begins with a loss, a death of the familiar: "Everywhere, no matter what the sphere of interest (whether religious, political, or personal), the really creative acts are represented as those deriving from some sort of dying to the world; and what happens in the interval of the hero's nonentity so that when he comes back as one reborn, made great and filled with creative power, mankind is also unanimous in declaring" (Campbell, [1949] 1969, p. 35).

In the monomyth, the hero brings back the means for the regeneration of the society as a whole. Organizational history unveils the heroes and heroines who introduced changes that have been regenerative for the organization or have had significant systemic impact. The revisiting of history submerges trustees in the cultural depths of the organization's life and recreates the classic journey of the hero, the organization's epic of change, and the universal stages of transition. Trustees are given the opportunity to see patterns, the recycling of issues, turning points, and if and how trustees and other significant individuals helped the organization to re-emerge stronger and better. They can see, perhaps for the first time, their institutional capacity and their shared "heroism" and responsibility during times of transition. Historical reflection and analysis evoke a collective wisdom that can regenerate an organization and also help it to contribute to a greater good.

The process of reviewing an organization's history is an encounter with its monomyth. It identifies events that precipitated change and threatened the natural order of things—times when the organization was separated from the comfortable and familiar and thrown into a period of disorientation. During these times, the organization moves through a cycle of death and rebirth and faces the gap between the idyllic portrait of itself and the reality of organizational life. Those in an organization who can acknowledge these gaps without being paralyzed by disillusionment and fear or without engaging in a frenzy of solutions are most likely the leaders who will be able to develop creative, ethical responses that will aid the rebirth and survival of the organization. Their responses will have a generativity that will ensure that the organization will be stronger and better positioned to undergo its next cycle of change. When organizational learnings from these cycles and transitions are understood and integrated, they can be used to position an organization to face the future responsibly. In order to do this, the leaders who hold an organization in trust must first be in touch with the organization's story and the depth of meaning in its history.

An example of an organization's discovery of its monomyth through history is illustrated by the experience of a repertory theater located in an urban area in the Midwest. The organization felt itself to be at a critical crevice in its seven-year history. Its capacity to sustain itself financially into the future appeared to be endangered because of major cutbacks in state and federal funding on which the organization had greatly depended. A major planning initiative by its sponsoring institution had precipitated an inquiry into whether the theater needed to continue to exist and, if so, in what form. Through depth education that included a thorough review and analysis of its history, the organization began to understand its monomyth and recognized the cycle of transition it was experiencing. Only when the trustees faced the question, "Should the theater die?" was it freed to use the lessons of the past so that it could emerge stronger and clearer about the organization's reason for being and the need to continue to exist. The board could ably articulate the organization's identity, clarified its relationship to the sponsoring institution, negotiated a long-term lease with another organization, and has begun seeking ways to become financially self-sufficient in the next decade. The trustees and staff also established a way to pool organizational resources and obtained advertising and marketing with other appropriate arts groups in the area that cut costs and helped create an environment of broad-based community support of the arts. Since the board's experience of depth education, it has expanded the organization's financial base and resources, improved the quality of its productions, and gained much greater visibility. Reclaiming its history helped the theater to reclaim its mission, identify its distinctiveness from other theater groups, determine its capacity to manage change, and inspire the leadership to face transition and future change.

Revealing the monomyth reveals as well an ongoing cycle of endings, transition, and new beginnings. William Bridges's book *Transitions: Making Sense of Life's Changes* describes this three-stage universal of change and transition. Organizations experience endings as a period of disengagement and a change in the context in which they have operated. Comfortable, predictable roles and behaviors no longer seem to fit, and previously held assumptions and perceptions are questioned. There can be a loss of self-definition and identity, and even a feeling of nonexistence. In this time there is a clearing away of the old—a signal that change is required and that a "time has come to look below the surface of what has been thought to be so" (Bridges, 1980, p. 101).

Organizations can spend considerable energy trying to ward off the experience of loss felt in this stage. Numerous books and articles address rejuvenation and renewal, but there are few processes or resources that help organizations deal with the experience of loss and feelings of grief that come during these periods of dying. We need effective ways to help boards discuss and determine whether the organization's difficulties are a signal to change or a time to consider seriously whether to remain in business. Both are deaths, though of different kinds. If death is viewed as final, then we will be tempted to abort the full cycle of transition and not enter into the contemplation and discussion described in the second stage as the neutral zone.

The neutral zone is an experience of loss and chaos. This state is indispensable to any new creation, for in chaos an organization can find the elements of what is necessary for a new beginning. Wisdom is needed for organization members to remind themselves that "it is only by returning for a time to the formlessness of the primal state that renewal can take place. The neutral zone is the only source of renewal that we all seek" (Bridges, 1980, p. 120).

The experience of transition is a state of things not fitting anymore, making it difficult, if not impossible, to return to a previous form of existence. In the neutral zone, beliefs and practices need realignment. Figuring out how new information can be integrated or determining how it might fit requires an uncomfortable reexamination of what was previously comfortable and predictable. If the organization can provide safe space for this level of discourse and self-examination, wrestling with what no longer fits and must now be discarded, of examining where it needs to go and needs to embrace, then it can move toward a state of reintegration. Putting the pieces back together again is not a simple task; reintegration and the emergence of the new identity will include some elements from the past and some from the present.

The state of reintegration is a time of returning to a feeling of permanence and stability again: the stage of re-creation. A new form of organizational coherence and capacity develops, and as it does, it heightens confidence that the organization can resume functioning with competence. The lessons learned from the past are evident in new initiatives and directions. There is a refamiliarization with the core beliefs and values and their place in the culture, and a level of comfort and predictability that allows those in the system to function with security and greater ease. It is important for an organization to experience this phase fully; too rapid a pace of change does not allow the process of reintegration and stabilization needed to be prepared to cope with future transition. These stages of transition are inevitable, but the responses to them are not; trustees of an organization can be helped to learn from past history to read the signs of transition and position the organization to manage it in the future. Lessons learned from history can provide the information needed for a board to effectively lead through other transitions.

Using the History Time Line

With instruction and guidance provided by a consultant, the organization creates a history time line. The time line, a visual symbol of organizational identity and a graphic representation of a culture within the context of a larger environment, is used through the depth education process.

An elite private school in the Midwest created a time line for its annual board orientation and training retreat. The creation and analysis of the time line revealed a clear picture of the school's contributions and priorities: academic excellence, emphasis on the arts, and preparation for community leadership. It also revealed an enduring ambivalence about inclusivity, especially students who were minorities or from a lower socioeconomic class than the majority of the school's students. The school's continuing puzzlement about its inability to attract these categories of students was explained in its history and exclusionary past. Although the school wanted to change, it was confronted with the vestiges of its remembered history (and its monomyth) in the wider community. And although it was extremely proud of its heritage and past accomplishments, the school was forced to face the community's perception of a culture of elitism and preferred homogeneity and an imperviousness to changing ethnic demographics. It is still undecided whether the school and its governance leaders will make a sustained and substantive effort to reach beyond a predominantly affluent group to a broader, move diverse community of students and staff who look different from the current majority and are equally talented and capable. The school's history revealed both strengths and weaknesses. The responses to the truths discovered will reveal whether the board will be liberated by history or held hostage by it.

The school has computerized and printed its time line for use by all trustees and staff. It is preparing for a major anniversary celebration and will use the time line to educate alumni and build community support.

An example of a comprehensive and well-developed time line that has served to make the significant connections between social and political events and issues and organizational impact and responses in the life of philanthropic organizations is one created for the 1997 conference of the Grantmakers for Children, Youth and Families. The time line begins in 2300 B.C. and moves through the 1990s. The last two decades are shown in Resource G. It is an excellent resource for organizations engaged in philanthropic activity to see their development in a larger context over time. It has been used to help organizations examine their own tradition of philanthropy and to analyze the effect on their grantmaking activities. More important, it has helped to launch substantive conversations within institutions about internal assumptions and practices and opened up the possibility of grantmakers doing their work in new ways.

In the process of examining history, trustees are reinforced in their skills of seeing the whole, of moving back and forth between the internal and external realms of an organization's life, grasping the complexity of the multiple levels of culture, interpreting the meaning of all of this, and using this knowledge and understanding to forecast the future and position the organization to respond to it. These are the capacities so valuable in trustees.

Having an attractive and readable time line is important, but what is far more important in depth education is discerning the meaning of the information and the stories generated. Once everyone has had a chance to share the recorded, observed, and remembered history of the organization, the primary task is to determine what it means and how these insights can be applied to help the organization. Trustees are responsible for the interpretation of historical information, for giving it meaning, and they come to understand how much this task is reliant on the extent and quality of data generated from all three sources of history. As the larger story unfolds in chronological order, the small, individual stories of trustees and staff are placed in context. When the organization is older than anyone's history of service on the board, the organization needs to involve former board members who are capable of telling the important founding and formative stories. In the shifting back and forth from the personal story to the institutional saga, board members learn to see the particular parts and the whole simultaneously. And they can see the interweaving of the individual story with the organization's and larger community's stories. The ability to see these connections and the multiple levels of reality are important elements in the reasoning and problem-solving skills of boards, and this exercise of discerning meaning helps trustees practice them.

Trustees struggle with some important questions in examining history: What does the history say about the identity of the organization and the deeply held beliefs and values over time? What does it reveal about the way the organization handles crisis and adversity? What does it indicate are the strengths and the weaknesses? What does it say about the past and current capacity of the organization?

The organizational history time line serves as both a visual invitation and a reminder to board members of the need for a whole and broader view and the need to be simultaneously "historian, analyst and prophet"—all characteristics of effective trustees (Greenleaf, 1977, p. 24). The conversation about history moves participants through time and evokes conversation that helps trustees see characteristics, issues, and patterns more clearly. Trustees create a solid foundation and knowledge base from which they can determine the strengths and challenges of the institution for whom they have accepted responsibility.

An example of the application and usefulness of this history time line to practical day-to-day issues can been seen in the case of a twenty-five-year old organization located in a predominantly rural area. Its mission is to provide in-home services to the adults and children with mental and physical disabilities. A group of its senior management staff and board members were given an orientation to depth education. Three months after the orientation, the group met in retreat for work in history, mission, publics, and the visioning portion of future. The group completed a shared vision for the future and identified broad goals, which were to be further developed. The consultants arranged for follow-up with the executive director and the management staff to help them complete the development of goals and translate them into a plan of action.

The organization had an established pattern in which staff did extensive work on their assignments but the board members usually did not complete their work. The consultants helped the board and staff examine the reasons for this and identified several: a heavy reliance by the board on staff, problems of communication between board members, and difficulty with the management of conflict and change. Over the next six months, the consultants assisted the organization's leadership in dealing with these issues. The procrastination of the board continued, although not to its original extent. The consultants, in analyzing the accumulated history of the organization and the knowledge gained in working with them, felt that historical amnesia was a significant part of the problem. Although the original orientation session had been valuable, it had not included a history of the board's functioning. A meeting was arranged with the executive director and board leadership, and after an assessment of the organization's strengths and challenges was conducted, the group decided a "return to history" session was needed. This session focused on the development of the board as much as it did on the organization and its programs. An analysis and understanding of the life cycle of the organization gave the board members a framework for understanding their own behavior and responsibilities. They began to see and discuss how staff driven the organization was without blaming or attacking anyone, and they were also able to discuss their dependency on the executive director. The executive director talked about the positive and the negative impact of the board's behavior on his performance. Most of the board members began to see what the long-term effect of their behavior could be on the organization and started to address issues of governance, administration, and structure with a new earnestness and directness.

The use of history as a method of surfacing and analyzing issues helped to ease the tensions and resistance in this group. During the process, board members spoke of their own individual histories in relationship to the life cycle of the organization, and many spoke passionately about the mission of the organization. The "return to history" session provided a helpful context within which the roles of the board and staff could be analyzed and the board could begin to address how it could function better. This board decided to set aside time at future meetings to have this level of discussion. The organization published a new brochure showcasing its history and using the theme of dreams.

The organization has now moved into the new facility it had once envisioned. The process of depth education was not the sole variable in bringing about the organization's purchase of a new facility, but it certainly helped board members to change their evaluation of the previous facility and to see its limitations in serving the organization's publics. It also altered the way the board perceived itself, its role, and its responsibilities, especially its responsibility for the long-term health of the organization.

One of the most important responsibilities of trustees is that of planning; a historical understanding is one of the key components in successful planning. Usually the process begins with a look at the current state of the organization, and this forms the basis for the establishment of future goals and objectives. But this approach often leads to uninspired planning and weak follow-through. Part of what is missing is the context for planning that only historical review can provide. Carl Dudley discovered that organizations that use history as a component in planning were energized and had a new capacity to complete their plan: "When historical reflection occurs, planning becomes not just a rational, analytical process but an affirmation of who the organization sees itself to be" (1990, p. 3). Such affirmation is essential to the life and direction of an organization; confusion over identity will lead to confusion over direction.

In effect, the organization's plan for the future is an outward manifestation of its perceived or hoped-for identity. And it is through the sharing of history, with its collection of stories and the coming together of diverse perceptions, that ownership of the organization is deepened and the capacity to honor the past yet liberate itself to see new ways of being is nurtured. History is also a significant way to address one of the most important questions that can be asked of an organization: Why does this organization exist? Whom does it serve? These are questions of mission.

Chapter Eleven

Understanding Our Mission

If there is a term more frequently used than *leadership,* it is probably *mission.* Unlike leadership, however, there is a greater consensus about the meaning and importance of mission. A diversity of organizations—churches, schools, businesses, government, and voluntary organizations—cite mission as an important element of success. Unfortunately, too much emphasis is usually placed on mission as a statement of a prescribed length, and all too often the final product is absent a preparatory conversation in which the substance and the deeper meaning underlying the words have been addressed, agreed on, and communicated.

There is little doubt that a clearly written, compelling statement of mission makes fundraising and marketing much easier; it does affect an organization's ability to generate and sustain voluntary and financial support. But mission is the center point in an organization. It cannot be reduced to being a marketing tool. A statement of mission, written and used without engaging in the depth exploration and discernment of calling and congruence, may jeopardize organizational credibility and financial solvency in the long term. Holding an organization in trust means having a commitment to taking time to probe into the center point—its core—and examining what is vital and of greatest value to an organization. A depth education of trustees facilitates an exploration of mission as the overarching reason for the organization's existence. This exploration is a continuation of the one initiated in history, now viewed through the lens of mission.

Why do we exist? What are we called to be? What are we called to do? Whom are we serving? These are the elemental questions that frame the discussion and discernment of mission. Depth education elicits an identification of the core beliefs and values of an organization, assesses how these are lived out in organizational behavior, policies, and programs, and examines their impact on those inside and outside the organization. The conversation about mission is an examination of what the organization believes and values, whom it serves, and what it does (see Figure 11.1). How does the organization's actions reflect what it says it believes? How does its espoused values get expressed behaviorally? Trustees who ask and answer these questions, so central to its core of being, are ensuring organizational congruence and integrity.

One of the most promising responses to a depth exploration and education process was that of a professor who engaged her master's and doctoral graduate students in a project to examine their university's mission and publics. The purpose of the project was to evaluate the influences of the past on the current life and status of the university, focusing on the period from 1915 to 1965. The information gathered was to be used for the education of faculty and trustees about the character of the institution they serve and its core values. Their research showed that the university had been a national leader in liberal arts education and in the curriculum reform movement and had influenced many other educational institutions. They also learned that the university had a

Figure 11.1. Mission: Calling and Congruence

long tradition of service-learning and was a pioneer of this philosophy and in the pedagogy of education. Discovering this information evoked a tremendous sense of pride in those affiliated with the school. It provided them a mantle of success and a legacy of innovative leadership that the professor expects will inspire the faculty and students to live out the mission with renewed energy.

The conversation about mission is one of the most important ones an organization can have. So much depends on knowledge and clarity of mission that if there are conflicts about it, an organization will have difficulty proceeding into the future with security or confidence. One of the reasons for the difficulty of this conversation is that it is attached to deep wells of emotion and passion. The courage to look out and into a changing societal landscape and to ask whether an organization still needs to exist (or if you are the right person for its board) can be a discomforting experience. These questions touch more than individual interests or organizational needs; they connect to the needs of those whom the organization directly serves and the needs of those in the larger community.

This is a challenging exercise for trustees because the answers to these questions may lead to disruption of a comfortable way of being and a familiar way of seeing. The organization's original calling is being evaluated in a different time and place, and while the initial answer was an inspiring "yes" that galvanized people and moved them to action, the answer this time could be different and may invite a different result. Those serving in positions of trusteeship prefer to be associated with an organization that is growing, not one in a stage of demise, and yet one of the most important functions of trusteeship is to determine the necessity and value of an organization. Without doing these, the mission is at risk of becoming a string of phrases untouched by human heart or a sterile paragraph on paper, ignored when serious choices are being made.

All organizations have a public persona, and the larger public's perception can translate into financial support and survival or oblivion and decline. This is a reality that cannot be discounted but cannot be allowed to dominate in the conversation on mission. This is not a marketing discussion but rather a time for going deeper and enabling the organization to see itself fully and honestly. An authentic conversation about mission will invite a board to consider both the private and public spheres in which the organization operates and to evaluate how the organization's reality matches up to the ideal. The mission conversation brings attention to the gap between the real and the ideal, the gap between the public persona and the reality of the organization's life. It is in this gap where tensions and fears reside and where trustees will need to engage in adaptive work to help the organization attain greater internal and external integrity. It is in this gap where the board examines the relationship between the organization's beliefs and values, whom it serves, and what it does. It is here that trustees identify where there are connections and disconnections, and decide the relevance and strength of the former and the response to the latter. This is hard and exciting work and essential if organizational integrity and community trust are to be sustained.

Board members who are introduced to the concept of mission as calling, overarching purpose, and the reason that the organization exists can use it as the standard and measure of organizational congruence and integrity to hold the organization in trust and help to ensure its continuing renewal. The essence and import of this are eloquently captured in the words of Robert Lynn (1984, p. 8):

> At the root of the creative institution is a shared sense of vocation or, if you prefer, a common calling. In both the Jewish and Christian traditions, the presence of calling is embraced as a gift. The consequences of that gift are evident in a corporate sense of identity and in a unifying loyalty to a set of purposes. If that root sense of mission either has died or is decaying, the whole institution will sooner or later be affected in every respect. Nothing can be more subtle or serious an ailment than this sort of root disease. But whenever an institution undergoes renewal, its new life often springs from a deepened commitment to its vocation.

This deepened commitment to vocation can result from a depth education in and exploration of three areas: the organization's beliefs and values, whom it serves, and what it does. Boards are asked to complete their responses to each of three phases: "We believe . . . ," "We serve . . . ," and "We do. . . . " Their answers reveal important information and generate stimulating conversation about organizational purpose and program. The real value of this activity comes from an examination of what the information means.

Previous work by the board may have resulted in the development of a well-crafted mission statement; now the board is being asked to examine this statement in the light of the organization's day-to-day reality. The review of history has grounded the board in the identity of the organization; the exploration of mission focuses on alignment at organizational and individual levels and calls into question the commitment at both levels to the larger purpose. This inquiry provokes a discernment of meaning and justification for being.

Just as individuals must encounter these very questions at some point in their lives in order to become whole and healthy, organizations too must undergo similar analysis and integrative work in order to achieve health and wholeness. Depth education provides a way for trustees to enter the private and the public spheres of an organization's life and see its strengths and challenges. In doing this work, they can help the organization to grow and develop.

Trustees are both architects and guardians of organizational mission. They examine and ensure an alignment between the organization's core beliefs and values, whom it serves, and what it does. The statement of mission that results from this conversation should be a statement of congruence between these elements. When there is not congruence, there is organizational distress— an imbalance in the system that diminishes the integrity of the organization. Staff and clients can feel dis-ease when these elements are not aligned. The following situation exemplifies this problem.

A suburban Lutheran congregation requested assistance to work with its Council of Elders and staff to increase their effectiveness and to develop a vision of ministry for the future. From the beginning, there was some concern about how well the core concepts of depth education could be translated for this culture. The organizational assessment uncovered a low level of trust among members of the congregation, which was a bigger problem than the initial concerns about interpretation of the language of depth education in a religious setting. Depth education involves considerable group interaction, but this group had little experience in being a group and felt anxious about openly discussing issues that might cause conflict or discomfort in others. The minister, who had recently been called by the congregation, was enthusiastic about the potential of the PLANT™ process and wanted help with getting the council and staff to bond and work together as a team.

The history session provided the group with an opportunity to begin to be cohesive and to experiment with new behavior in a climate of safety. During the time line activity, everyone's story was seen as important in developing the whole history. Members began to feel increased trust, a greater sense of a shared experience, and more comfort in talking to one another. During the process, the group discovered that the area of mission was the most problematical for them, and they requested additional time and assistance from the consultants. As they expressed it, "We've not ever touched on such deep matters of the heart." Another half-day session resulted in deeper conversation about matters of the heart, from which a statement of mission emerged with which the group felt comfortable. But the work was challenging and uncomfortable.

The group's struggle with mission revealed a simmering conflict over diversity in their membership and lifted up an issue that needed further work. They were able to move forward, establishing a focus and direction for programs in the intermediate future that were congruent with their current mission. There was recognition that incongruence still existed between their beliefs and actions in the area of diversity of membership and that continued work needed to occur on whom they directly serve. The consultants felt it wise for the group to take some time to integrate their new learnings, develop more skill in working together as a group, and practice consensus decision making as preparation for their continued work in mission.

This organization is an example of the importance of coming to consensus about why an organization exists. And it also shows that sometimes the reason for apparent organizational peace (or lethargy) can be avoidance of a conversation about the core beliefs and values that drive the organization's decisions and give it its distinctive identity. Dissonance in the elements of mission can create organizational drag, weighing the organization down in such a way that creative solutions cannot take flight.

Discussions about mission can bring to the surface emotions, passions, and conflicts that many groups feel ill equipped to handle. In this case, the consultants brought a sensitivity to the situation, an understanding and respect for the culture, and a recognition of the organization's norms about change. At the same time, they encouraged the group to confront risk and helped to nurture the seeds of ongoing self-reflection and evaluation. To have done otherwise might have meant a reinforcement of group retreat and a flight from dealing directly with issues that are central to the organization's character. This organization's exposure to the concept of trusteeship through depth education helped to move it to a state of increased congruence in what is going to be a long process of transition. Once the trustees have conversed about and considered the full scope and overarching meaning of mission, they will reexamine their mission statement and conduct a mission audit to ensure congruence.

In order for an organization to answer the critical questions posed in the conversation about mission, it must understand what is meant by "We serve. . . . " To serve one's publics truly requires an openness to and an understanding of their needs. This means having the ability to listen deeply and to read both words and behavior, understanding what is obvious and what is implied. Needs are not discerned or defined in a vacuum; they emerge from past and current understanding and processing of gathering data. The organization's style and tradition of identifying and responding to identified needs are reflective of community standards, ethics, and norms for the kind of life we want for all people. In a significant way, we are talking about an organization's participation in the expression of a moral and ethical conversation about our relationship to one another, to community, and to society as a whole. Trustees who engage in this complex conversation and thought and who perceive this level of connectedness and accountability between provider and recipient can inspire and support the development of policies that enable staff to provide and sustain appropriate and effective programs over the long term.

The very process of answering questions about client needs and what it means to serve helps boards to continue to define the agency's primary clients and to establish clear accountability and appropriate boundaries of outreach. The board is better able to see the organization's served publics in the context of a larger community as well. Perhaps if more organizations could attain this view, collaboration would be much easier. In depth education, trustees are taught to view and respond to the organization in the context, so that its assessment is not limited to what is obvious or individually determined, and sociocultural, economic, and political factors can be considered before deciding on the proper action. Boards that adopt the practice of seeing the organization in the situation can use the big-picture lens that is so necessary for visualizing creative, relevant programs and for visualizing an organization's future.

One vital and essential ingredient that enables trustees to risk the level of honesty, self-scrutiny, and judgment inherent in depth education is trust—trust gained through a shared history and commitment to a larger purpose. This commitment and an understanding of public need and accountability enable the capacity to build the trust that is essential to take future risks.

The connections between the personal mission of board members and the mission of the organization deserve attention also. Board members need to examine their own beliefs and values and determine how these interact with those of the organization. This discussion not only helps link them to a larger purpose; it becomes the foundation for determining their personal stake in the organization: what they are willing to commit to do or invest in and what they will be responsible for during their tenure.

The understanding of personal mission and organizational mission intersects in ways that affect the contribution that board members can make to the organization. In our work with individuals and organizations, we have experienced various combinations of personal and organizational mission and the effect these have on an individual's ability to contribute to a board. The model in Figure 11.2 depicts four significant ways these can come together and can serve to help organizations and trustees decide where they are best suited to serve and in what capacity.

Marginal members are those who lack a sense of their own mission and are on the board of an organization whose mission may be unclear or in need of change. They are disconnected to the organization and feel at the edge of things. This disconnection may be perceived as passivity or lethargy and results in a form of marginalism. If the reason they were selected for board service is their status, wealth, and name recognition, they can still experience a form of isolation.

A socially prominent and wealthy woman was in high demand for board service. She was eager to volunteer her time and generous in her financial support to those organizations on whose boards she served. Prior to being married, she had had a highly responsible job that required administrative skill and political savvy, but few of the

Figure 11.2. Relationship of Mission to Board Service

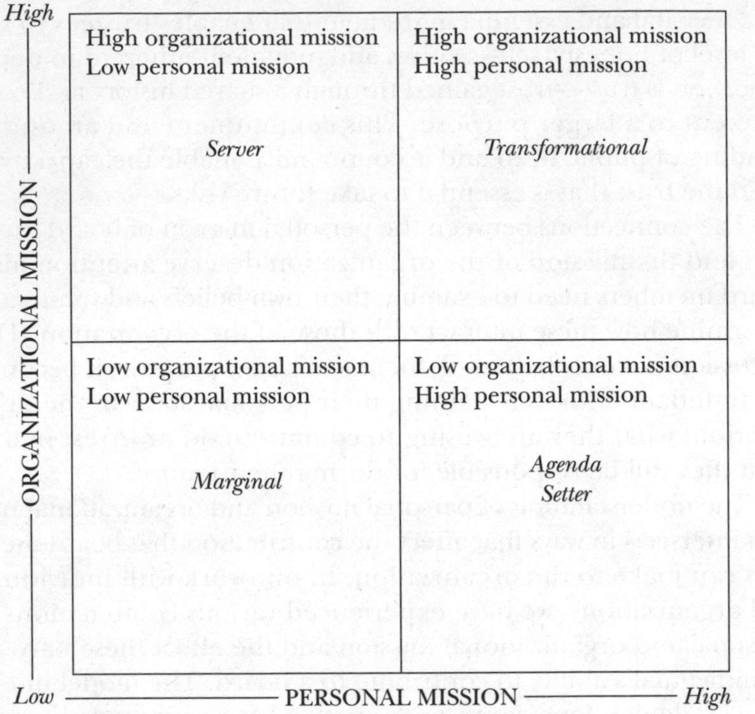

<table>
<tr><td>High organizational mission
Low personal mission

Server</td><td>High organizational mission
High personal mission

Transformational</td></tr>
<tr><td>Low organizational mission
Low personal mission

Marginal</td><td>Low organizational mission
High personal mission

*Agenda
Setter*</td></tr>
</table>

ORGANIZATIONAL MISSION (vertical axis, *High* to *Low*)

Low ———————— PERSONAL MISSION ———————— *High*

organizations recruiting her seemed to know about or acknowledge these capacities. The focus of her involvement was mainly on the money she could contribute, and this confined her to a position in which she was treated deferentially and not expected to attend all board or committee meetings. Her inner being was not engaged or cultivated in ways that encouraged growth. Ironically, although she was perceived as important, she ended up feeling devalued. Before moving to another community, she shared her disappointment in these kinds of voluntary experiences.

Agenda setters feel clear about their own sense of personal mission. When they are in a situation in which the organization is questioning or confused about mission, they tend to move quickly toward resolution. Organizations need leaders who can commit to action, but agenda setters have a low tolerance for ambivalence or ambiguity and may drive the organizational agenda with their own agendas, allowing their core beliefs and values to dictate organizational decisions and direction. In effect, their personal mission can supersede the mission of an organization. Organizations in states of transition whose identity is being debated may be at higher risk with members like this unless they can be helped to separate self-interest from organizational interests.

The not-for-profit sector is a place where private aspirations and public needs can combine to serve the common good and to achieve something greater than could be accomplished otherwise. Whatever the individual passion or unique gift offered in board service, it is best exercised in concert with the larger purpose of the organization.

The board of a counseling center panicked when the vice president who was soon to be elected president resigned, and they hurriedly elected an individual who had been a client and had served on the board less than a year. The new president's comprehension of the history of the organization was limited and was primarily through her personal experience of being a recipient of services. Her individual passion to serve battered women became the organization's highest programmatic priority, although the organization's mission was to serve a broader constituency. In less than two years under her leadership, the organization became known for its services to victims of domestic violence rather than a comprehensive community resource center for women.

Individuals driven by personal mission are valuable in starting something new and inspiring others to action. Their tendency to impose what they believe onto situations can be both positional and negative. If they can be helped to broaden their perspective, channel their passions, and check for congruence between their beliefs and the core beliefs of the organization, they can be highly constructive and powerful leaders in carrying out the purposes of the organization.

Servers are those who have a clarity about the organization's mission and a dedication to helping the organization respond effectively to those it exists to serve. Their understanding of their own personal mission is not particularly strong, and this can significantly narrow the contributions that they make to an organization. Servers are valuable contributors to an organization's capacity to be accessible and caring. If there is no ongoing reexamination of organizational mission, they can contribute to perpetuating programs that have outlived their usefulness. The creativity, energy, and ideas or new thinking that can challenge direction or stimulate an organization's imagination can become calcified. Servers can be a wonderful source of support for direct services and hands-on experiences, but without an inner compass to help guide them in depth conversations and decision making, they can have difficulty setting boundaries or achieving balance between ensuring future organizational stability and meeting immediate needs.

Transformational leaders hold their personal mission and an organization's mission together, seeing how they overlap at the core, yet they remain clear about when it is appropriate to challenge their growth and that of an organization. They maximize the capacities and gifts they bring and apply them toward the greater good of the organization. They model the balance between self-interest and the common good and feel affirmed in their purpose while helping to fulfill the mission of the organization. Boards that have members with a clear sense of their own core values and beliefs, a sense of whom they are called to serve, and a full understanding of the relationship of personal mission to the mission of the organization bring a depth of commitment and leadership that inspires and sustains those who are connected to the organization. Transformational leaders model congruence and connection. They are empathic with those whose lives are directly touched by the organization and can negotiate clear boundaries between direct service and their governance and policy-setting responsibilities.

Those considering board service need to be given opportunities to educate themselves about their personal mission and an organization's mission. Assistance in determining their affinity with an organization's core beliefs and values, those it serves, what it does, and what it envisions for its future are key to the development of trustee commitment. Organizations can begin to educate leaders so they are able to discover the overlap between personal and organizational calling. In this overlap can be found the fertile ground for deeper commitment. Getting leaders to find this place in their lives is a part of depth education for trusteeship. It is part of the inner work of leadership, and it serves as a rite of passage in the development of trustees who will be able to hold an organization in trust through change and transition. Organizations with strong, competent boards of trustees know there are no shortcuts to searching for and preparing those who will be responsible for the future of the organization. The cultivation of a cohesive, committed, competent board with a "generosity of spirit," as one trustee described it, is an investment with high returns.

Before becoming members, prospective trustees can be asked questions that help them to decide whether their involvement is a fit for them and for the organization. The right questions and opportunities for reflection can lead to greater clarity of purpose and a stronger, deeply committed group. Following are some questions that can be used to help prospective trustees make these connections:

1. When and how did you first become involved in volunteering?
2. What was your first volunteer experience? Who involved you? What did you do? What was the result?
3. What have been your subsequent board and community service experiences?
4. What was most satisfying about your previous board experiences? Why? What was least satisfactory? Why?
5. What would you say are the core beliefs and values of this organization?
6. How do they appeal to your core beliefs and values?
7. What is the relationship between your answers to questions 5 and 6?
8. How do you see yourself contributing to this organization?
9. What is there about this organization that excites you?
10. What is there about this organization that concerns you?
11. What are the three most important things you want to learn during your experience as a board member?
12. What are the three most important gifts you want to give to this organization?

These questions or similar ones can be used to screen and select trustees, and they can provide valuable information about how to design an orientation for new trustees. The process of questioning also conveys a serious commitment to the organization and to the development of its trustees.

The history time line process can be used in the discernment of personal mission. Trustees can be asked to recall and record their experiences of voluntarism and to see what the common themes are. In examining their previous and current acts of service, board members are reconnected to what calls them, what brings them joy and satisfaction, and what inspires their commitment and their caring for others. They can begin to identify connecting values and use what is important to them in making decisions about future service. This kind of knowledge enables trustees to serve and to lead in organizations where there is a strong connection to their own sense of mission.

Chapter Twelve

Understanding the Publics We Serve

Publics are defined as the individuals and institutions with whom an organization is in relationship. These relationships can involve direct service, collaboration, or service exchange. They constitute a network that can aid or hinder the organization's ability to carry out its mission. A review of publics extends the conversation begun in mission and moves the organization into exploration of a larger arena. Boundaries of organizational service can be examined and renegotiated as necessary. A review of publics defines the organization's universe, and the self-portrait that emerged in mission can now be held up for greater scrutiny and checked against the perceptions of those external to the organization. In many ways, the conversation about publics is one of asking an organization to draw a map of its universe and to see itself as if for the first time. This provides trustees with a fresh look at what is familiar. The portrait can enable an organization to see itself in context and see patterns of change and whether or how it needs to change. It also can help trustees to examine whether and how well they are living out their responsibility to serve as organizational educators to the larger community and to determine whether they are accurately and effectively articulating the mission to the larger community. An organization exists in a context, not in a vacuum, and its trustees are responsible for being aware of what it looks like, how it is changing, and what the effects of these changes may mean for the organization. An exploration of an organization's publics gives the trustees the information necessary to use in their reading of reality.

Historical and mission reflection teaches trustees how and why the organization came into existence and reveals its phases of development. Examining publics raises questions of relationship and connectedness and helps an organization identify real and potential allies and enemies. Who else cares about and should know about this organization? and Who is missing at our table? are additional questions that need to be addressed. At this juncture in depth education, boards experience a notable change in the scope and focus of the conversation, one similar to the change in perception of the earth when humans first landed on the moon. The way we viewed the earth and our understanding of our relationship to and for it was dramatically altered after seeing the swirling blue and white ball suspended in a deep, ink-black, star-sprinkled night. We knew that the earth is round and part of a vast galaxy, but until that breathtaking sight in 1969, we lacked the perspective to comprehend fully its beauty, fragility, and interconnectedness to a much larger system. From that time forward, our place on earth and our interdependence with its other inhabitants was powerfully different. From our place on the earth, it had seemed vast, almost infinite; now it appears finite, and the need to protect and preserve it for the future—to hold it in trust—has a new and compelling urgency. We realize that earth's survival is literally in our hands—in the hands of all of its inhabitants—and that a partnership between nature and human beings is necessary if earth is to continue to be a habitable, life-giving home.

Seeing an organization from a different perspective may or may not have as dramatic an impact as the view of the whole earth from the moon has had, but providing ways for trustees to step outside the organization and to see it from a different vantage point and through the eye of others is an experience of seeing the organization whole that can change trustees' perspectives about the organization they serve and their responsibility and connection to the greater community. An exploration of publics provides some distance and encourages new perspectives.

Depth education engages board members in an analysis of the organization's publics and how they have changed over time. The founding and formative events in an organization's life are reminders to governance and staff leaders that the organization was conceived in response to a public need within a community. During the conversation regarding publics, trustees are invited to look at the complex interplay between the organization and community and to view the organization as a part of a vast web of relationships. This part of depth education enlarges the trustees' view of the organization and its interdependence on and relationship to this network. A depth examination of the organization and of the community in which it lives can serve to minimize organizational tendencies toward isolationism and insularity, and can make it amenable to possibilities of collaboration and partnership.

Asking the question, Whom do we exist to serve? gives trustees an opportunity to talk about the recipients of its services. The question, In what context? moves the organization and its trustees into a realm of accountability and community that will not allow it to become complacent. The organization's environmental map or universe will change, and the trustee leaders will strive for accuracy and completeness in their reading and interpretation. In this conversation, trustees are reminded that they are trustees of the larger community and that the organization is accountable to the larger community through them.

Several more questions can broaden the organization's perception as it looks beyond itself and those directly affected by its service: Whom does the organization need to be in relationship with in order to serve these publics? How can the organization expand its awareness of a wider community? How can it initiate and sustain dialogue with the larger community? How can it respond best to competing claims as well as the opportunities for collaboration that awareness of a larger community brings? The process of answering these questions is valuable depth work for trustees, for they are responsible for clearly defining the organization's boundaries of outreach and accountability and prioritizing whom it will serve. These are difficult but essential responsibilities if the organization's capacity to serve is going to be improved.

To facilitate this conversation and level of exploration, we define publics in three different ways:

Publics served. The publics an organization serves are the primary recipients of the organization's programs and resources, such as time, money, and staff—for example, the children who participate in an after-school program at a child care center.

Publics attended. The publics attended are those individuals, groups, and organizations that are the secondary recipients of an organization's resources and whose involvement with and relationship to the organization has a direct effect on the organization's capability to serve its primary publics—for example, funders, vendors, other service delivery organizations.

Publics considered. The publics considered are individuals, groups, and organizations that are members of the larger community and are given thought and regard as the organization engages in planning and decision making—for example, non-youth-serving organizations that offer after-school programs, youth who are not receiving services in the community, law enforcement agencies, schools, businesses, and civic groups.

Every organization is part of a complex galaxy of service systems and a network of publics in a community. Some of these publics are essential to the organization's existence, while others are peripheral and have little or no effect. It is the responsibility of trustees to identify the organization's advocates and adversaries, its collaborators and competitors, its supporters and the oblivious. After clarifying its publics and what relationship it chooses to have with them, a determination can be made about who among board and staff is responsible for cultivating communication and relationships with these specific publics.

In working with organizations, we help them to draw a picture of their publics, using a model that shows the degree of connection with these publics and the importance of trustees' establishing parameters of service so that the organization can focus and deploy its resources strategically (see Figure 12.1). The concentric circles are used to help boards define those publics that are closest to their organization and to which their resources are aimed, as well as other publics without which it would be difficult to accomplish their mission. The figure also imparts the message that trustees have a responsibility to set boundaries appropriate to the mission and considerate of the resources the organization possesses. In this discussion, trustees are invited to research and talk with the organization's publics, to listen to them and get their understanding of what the organization is and what it does or does not do. This is an opportunity for the organization to see itself "from the moon" and to see what other orbits are encircling its space. Hearing the different perspectives of clients and strangers, friends and enemies, can help the organization decide if and how it needs to respond differently, and it can then do so with the advantage of seeing a comprehensive picture.

This exploration and discussion is an important way for the organization to connect to the intricate community in which it resides. Part of the value of this approach is that it leads to an assessment and vision of the kind and quality of relationships that the organization seeks and a determination of who among the staff and the board will assume responsibility for tending the relationships with these publics. The board and staff can assume the ongoing tasks of developing and ensuring that there are structures of communication in place that will provide the organization with current and accurate information from its publics and alert it to changes in the larger environment that the organization needs to know. Without such information, the capacity to project ahead will be impaired. The ability to read the context and relate to the larger community affects the way the board and staff function together in their management and leadership of an organization.

Figure 12.1. An Organization's Publics

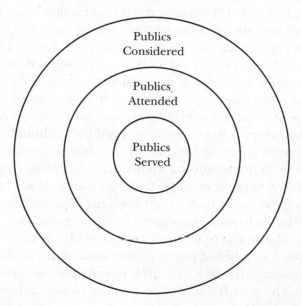

The conversation about publics reminds trustees of their responsibilities to be both educators and advocates. Having a development officer or expert in marketing and public relations on staff will not absolve trustees of their responsibility to "tell and sell." Board members are sometimes surprised at how little people know about the organizations they serve, and they may forget what a valuable resource they themselves are in explaining to the community what their organization does. Trustees are responsible for keeping the community informed about the organization and can be the most influential articulators of how the organization is achieving its mission and accomplishing its goals. They communicate whether and how community needs are being addressed, and they are able to ascertain new needs and position their organization to meet them. Keeping informed about changing needs and the effects of these on an organization is an important board responsibility. A continuing conversation about publics reinforces the board's capacity to educate and influence the organization's universe.

A large parish located in the heart of a thriving city began to raise questions about how it could expand and strengthen its mission "beyond the walls" and asked for assistance in addressing this challenge through engaging in long-range planning. In preparation for this work, the resource committee adapted the PLANT™ questionnaires called "Learning from Our Publics" (see Resource H) and conducted interviews with community and religious leaders, members of their parish, and citizens at large. They then shared their findings with each other and discussed what the information meant. This was the first time the parish had been intentional about listening to those they thought they were serving, and they were surprised at how little those interviewed knew about their philanthropic efforts in the community. Although everyone they spoke with knew the location of the church, few knew its correct name or denominational identity or what programs and services it offered to those outside its congregation. Many of those in the congregation were unaware of the generous contributions the parish had made to numerous social service organizations and civic initiatives. The resource committee learned from surveys and interviews that a number of young professional adults working in the business community were in search of spiritual nurture and revitalization. The parish decided to provide opportunities for luncheon discussion groups and to be more aggressive in marketing these offerings. Recognition of the potential for service equipped the parish with a better understanding of how it was perceived and helped it to rethink its educational offerings and strategies for dissemination to a broader audience. Although it had been sobered by the initial feedback, the parish moved constructively to close the gap between its original intent and the actual impact of its activities and responded with a creative outreach program.

An organization comes into being at a particular time in history and develops from a particular sense of what the founders believe is needed to respond to a particular problem. The same kind of reading and responsiveness is needed from current and future trustees. The external environment is continually changing, and unless the trustees are aware of these changes, the organization may find itself in an entirely different environment yet still doing what it has always done. The question of whether it is still appropriate to do what has always been done is revisited during the discussion about publics, and the answers should derive from a depth conversation that balances the need for an organization to retain stability and integrity while responding to emerging client and community needs.

If board members are to become transformational leaders, they will need to possess a knowledge of the vast circle of people and organizations that circumscribe and affect the organization and on whom the organization has influence. The discussion about publics is an opportunity for the trustees of an organization to create context and community within which wiser decisions about future service can be made. The following example demonstrates the impact of enlarging an organization's definition of publics.

A planning agency for social agencies located in a predominantly rural southern county requested assistance in developing a strategic plan. The area was experiencing rapid growth and an increased strain on its already burdened service delivery system. The executive director, board president, key staff, and board members met with two consultants who oriented them to the depth education process. The board decided to proceed, and over several months its resource committee prepared for a two-day retreat during which board members, key staff, and representatives from the community participated. After going through history, mission, publics, and the visioning portion of future, the board appointed a task force to develop the final strategic long-range plan. The consultants who facilitated the retreat were retained to assist in the development of this plan, and they periodically met with the task force over the next year. The group conducted interviews and surveys with a variety of persons in the community about their perceptions, expectations, and suggestions for the future of the organization.

The full board was intermittently informed of the task force's progress, and it approved the final draft of the plan at a board meeting a year after the initial retreat. The five-year strategic plan was unveiled to the community at a highly publicized annual meeting through an informative slide presentation and new brochure, both highlighting the work accomplished in depth conversations and decision making about history, mission, publics, and future. The organization described the plan as a living document that will continue to be influenced by those they serve directly and those in the larger community. The community feels in partnership with this organization and has a stake in its success.

Implicit in this example is a concern for and belief in the common good. To any shared undertaking, trustees bring varying beliefs, values, and opinions about what is best for a community. They act as a permeable membrane, transmitting the needs of the community to the organization and interpreting the knowledge, identity, and activities of the organization to the community. In this way, their decision making occurs within the context of the whole community. Trustees link organization and community, ensuring accountability, responsiveness, and credibility.

This approach prevents the "frog in hot water" phenomenon that can occur when an organization has not paid sufficient attention to external changes and the potential impact these can have on it. The strong traditions of an organization can lull a board into a false sense of security that dulls the ability to comprehend fully the risks and opportunities surrounding it.

A Lutheran children's home whose origins date back to the Civil War era sought help in developing a long-range plan. The organizational assessment revealed a priority need to revisit the mission. The full dialogue of historical reflection, mission discernment, and connecting with its publics helped the board to understand the importance of depth education if the organization was going to have any chance of surviving into the next century. During the process, the trustees learned that the original reason for the organization's existence was no longer in effect. It had originally been created to serve orphans, but over time it began to admit children with different needs, and it now predominantly serves emotionally disturbed children. The organization's infrastructure was ill equipped to handle this new population. The lack of attention to this change had contributed to high staff turnover, low morale, and a decreased capacity to handle increasingly serious behavioral problems in clients. The board could clearly see the misfit between the internal organizational capacity and the needs of its new publics.

Another major transition confronting this organization was the impending retirement of the executive director after nearly three decades of leadership. There had not been any planning for transition, and the board suddenly realized the difficulty. The history session introduced the board to the discipline of data collection and anticipation and identification of future issues and trends. They gained insights and learnings from the past and saw both the mistakes and wisdom of those who had preceded them. As a result, they began to think about the consequences of their own behavior and decision making and their impact on the life and future of the organization. This organization is experiencing major changes and transitions, and its board is now better positioned to manage them.

Boards of organizations are responsible for holding not only the organization in trust, but for holding the community in trust as well. They represent the interests of the organization and of the community. They are responsible for communicating what the organization is and what it does for the larger community. Trustees assure a community that the organization they govern is viable, has integrity, and is financially and programmatically sound. Reciprocally, trustees are also responsible for bringing the issues and concerns of the larger community to the organization's discussions and decision making. They must consider the entire community, and the myriad and often competing claims on its resources. These responsibilities of trust holding are great. A board's capacity to carry them out effectively evolves from a deeper understanding of the variety of its publics and its relationship and responsibility to them.

Chapter Thirteen

Building Our Future Together

The future is the next conversation in depth education; usually, though, it is the first thing that boards ask for assistance with. More commonly referred to as strategic long-range planning, it prepares a governing body to anticipate and project the organization's work and growth into the future. Planning is a skill with which most boards are familiar; their professional jobs and educational backgrounds have prepared many of them to exercise this skill. The framework for this planning process is the knowledge acquired in history, mission, and publics. Trusteeship of an organization requires a depth understanding of its past *and* the ability to imagine its preferred future. The session on future helps trustees to accomplish this by visioning first and then translating the vision into action. Visioning engages trustees in developing a future portrait of the organization and enables them to establish goals, objectives, strategies, tasks, and time lines to achieve this vision.

Asking trustees to plan without depth education and preparation is a lot like asking someone with limited or no knowledge of the composition of the soil, the necessary nutrients for growth, the proper climate, or the environment to plant a tree. To increase the chances for the tree to prosper, the gardener must be aware of and attend to all of these elements. Similarly, organizational growth and stability depend on governance and program leaders who have a strong understanding of the organization and the larger environment in which it is rooted and in which it will need to adapt in order to grow in the future.

The depth education process does not revert to the present as the beginning point for planning. Research conducted by Ronald Lippitt at the University of Michigan has shown that using current reality as the starting place for future planning diminishes a group's energy and its capacity to envision. It also tends to lessen the board's grasp of issues and problems and its ownership in effectively implementing the final plan. Too many planning documents sit on shelves collecting dust; the main reason is the lack of ownership. Depth education reinforces appropriate ownership of a board's role in achieving the vision for the future.

To envision the future and position the organization to respond responsibly, trustees need to remove themselves temporarily from the present and journey to the future, to dream with inspiration and confidence about the ways the organization's mission can be lived out in different circumstances and with changing needs, neither of which can be predicted but must be anticipated. It is truly an organic process requiring considerable work and adaptive ability. As Parker Palmer reminds us (1990, p. 10), "The future of an organization depends not on rational planning but on an organic capacity to adapt to whatever comes along—without losing its integrity." Effective trustees have a capacity to dream beyond what exists in the here and now, and can then help to translate that dream or preferred image of the future into a specific plan of action. They know that planning for the future is not the same as being in control of it. Having been deeply grounded in the organization's past and present, the board is now asked to use this rootedness to help the organization break new ground and to grow in new ways.

Depth education gives trustees an opportunity to visualize what can be. They can engage in a guided imagery exercise specifically designed for their organization, during which they imagine the organization in the next ten to fifteen years. Their images are shared and translated into common themes, which are then put together to create a common portrait of the future of the organization. Once the future portrait is agreed on, the trustees are asked to reexamine the vision they have created, using the lessons and learnings derived from the organization's character, culture, calling, and context. This helps them to determine whether their image of the organization's future accurately reflects identity, purpose, service, and publics. The motivating forces for envisioning and planning for the future become ones of creation and transformation rather than reaction and correction. Organizations need trustees with a capacity to dream, a shared vision, and the will and courage to risk translating it into action. Envisioning is as valuable a skill as the ability to read a financial statement.

A major metropolitan parks department board in a Northwest city dared to dream about the use of underdeveloped properties in its city and undertook a depth planning process to make it a reality. After board members completed their own depth education experience, they developed and disseminated a booklet to the community with the vision that the board had created for the park. The vision was presented in the form of pictures and prose, and members of the community were issued an invitation to respond and help develop it further. The booklet shared four landmark beliefs on which the park system has come to be based and that framed the emerging vision. After hearing from the larger public, the board integrated what they heard, decided on a final version of the vision, and developed and oversaw the implementation of the plan to make the vision a reality. The result of this process is a beautiful, well-landscaped parks system for the city with bike and walking paths, picnic areas, and adequately equipped areas for rest and recreation—truly hospitable space for all age groups in the community.

Providing trustees with a process that engages them in visualization based on depth planning provides solid footing for the long-term stability of an organization. Another example of an agency that used depth education as a foundation for planning is that of a twenty-year-old inner-city agency that serves young adolescent boys. The planning process was a response to a request from the major funder and was part of the process of obtaining grant assistance. The board was composed primarily of independent entrepreneurs and corporate executives who were quite reliant on the executive director for direction. The executive director, a male in his late forties, had been with the organization since its inception. The typical style of board communication was one-to-one conversation with the executive director. Most substantive discussion and decision making was handled in the executive committee meetings, and rarely did board members feel the need to be present at board meetings. However, there was nearly 100 percent attendance at all program celebrations and fundraising events. By everyone's account, the organization was highly successful.

The staff had recently completed an agency service delivery evaluation and had collected extensive data about clients and programs. This information caused them some concern about the organization's staffing capacity to meet the needs of their primary clients in the future. This uneasiness, coupled with pressure to develop a plan, affected their motivation to try depth education. They were informed that this process would prepare them to complete a plan and that it required full board participation.

After an organizational assessment and the board's commitment to participate, an orientation was held, introducing the board and key staff to the concept of holding in trust. A resource committee was selected, and four half-day sessions were scheduled over the next six months to focus on four elements of depth education: history, mission, publics, and the visioning portion of future. These formal educational sessions were followed by a one-day board retreat focusing on the planning portion of future in which the strategic plan would begin to be developed. Over the course of the following year, the consultants worked with small subgroups of board and staff, each with assigned goals for development. The planning process took a year and a half (the illness of a key member extended the time line), but this is also a culture that moves deliberately and methodically in its decision making. In addition, this organization reviewed its board structure, identified and formed new committees, and gave expanded assignments to already established committees. It continued to work with a consultant to develop orientation materials for new board members.

The organization's board was revitalized and focused toward a shared purpose and direction. The executive director now feels that the board members have reconnected with their original reasons for volunteering, and they are now looking ahead and beginning to work as a group that grasps what it means to hold the organization in trust.

The visioning and planning sessions integrate the previous depth work done by a board and help trustees to create a picture of the organization that is grounded in solid data yet has space for the new and the unknown. The vision is translated into goals and objectives, tasks and time lines, and each goal will serve to accomplish the vision. Each goal is analyzed, and a determination is made about its appropriateness and feasibility; then a recommendation is made about whether the organization can strengthen the enabling forces and minimize the hindering forces sufficient to pursue the goal. There is rich discussion that leads to board concurrence on which goals are relevant and achievable. This process not only helps trustees determine what is reasonable for the organization to achieve, but specifies in what time span and determines whether the decisions and plans made are congruent with the organization's mission. Before the plan is finally approved by the board, a "mission check" is conducted to determine if the goals are congruent with the core values and beliefs of the organization. Once this is done, the plan is ready for implementation.

In a medium-sized southern city the chamber of commerce board went through the visioning process in one of several depth education retreats. The group reached consensus on the vision to build a new convention center. The business community had identified this as a need for a number of years, but could never get the agreement and support necessary to complete such a huge project. The process generated such commitment and a sense of holding the community in trust that these retreats are credited with moving this project forward. After the planning retreat in which the vision was defined, a team of chamber members quickly revived previous efforts to secure a hotel that would anchor the project. The city now has a beautiful $37 million civic center. More important is the core group of leaders representing nearly all sectors, who see themselves as trustees of their community.

One of the most important ways to help to improve governance leadership in organizations is to view and conduct board education as leadership development. Then organizations will be able to value the usefulness of these concepts well beyond a retreat or consultation. The completion of the strategic plan, decision making, and board development are important leadership tasks and warrant ongoing attention and continuing education. Most of the organizations that have engaged in the depth education process require more time to complete a strategic plan than is allowed for in a retreat that lasts one and a half or two days. We discovered that just at the point when staff and trustees were translating their vision into action, the services of the consultants would be terminated. Yet this is a critical time for most organizations engaged in depth education. The expectations and energy are high, but the detailed work ahead saps some of the energy unless the tasks are continually linked to the previous work and the shared vision.

When we surveyed these organizations to find out what they were most in need of, they overwhelmingly identified assistance with developing the details of a plan. They were not referring to just the sometimes tedious tasks of deciding and recording who will do what and when; they meant the cultural transition and shift in behavior that was now necessary to hold the organization in trust—that is, the need to change deeply ingrained communication patterns and practices that may no longer fit. Even organizations with a history of sophisticated planning and monitoring systems voiced a need for some form of sustained help in making the transition from vision to action.

Evaluating depth education is an important part of the process. Although board members and staff may feel a new sense of empowerment as trustees in this process, they have a short history of this new way of being. At the end of the experience of depth education, there are new questions and more choices—choices about continued planning, the structure and distribution of power, the composition of the board, the board's relationship to staff, norms for group functioning, their manner of decision making, and the integration of trustee education into the ongoing life and work of the board and organization. There may be a sense of vulnerability intertwined with celebratory feelings. This can be a difficult and uncomfortable time for some organizations, and continued assistance in various forms can be helpful. Follow-up in the areas of long-range planning, recruitment, orientation of new board members, renewal education for veteran board members, creating a culture of trusteeship, and teaching the board the practices of ongoing evaluation and education are all useful.

In short, this is an important transition in the development of trusteeship and leadership in an organization. The trustees are preparing to take on increased responsibility for their own development and the development of future trustees of the organization. The roles and responsibilities of staff may need renegotiation, and the consultant may need to assist with this work. Whatever the final arrangement is, the consultant needs to reinforce the idea that the organization is engaged in a continuing process of leadership education and development, and that it is the ultimate responsibility of a board to make this a normative process.

A young East Coast arts organization sought help with developing its board of directors into a group of leaders who would hold the arts and the organization in trust. Although the organization was several years old, it had no governance group until recent public funding became available to it. The organizational assessment and the individual and corporate storytelling identified characteristics of the culture that made it resistant to having a board, although one was legally required and fiscally essential. The founding staff and trustees carried strong beliefs about creativity, freedom, flexibility, and excellence that made them question whether their growth and maturity as an organization would now be dictated by structures and systems of accountability that would undermine these elements. The unspoken fears about this potential loss created an undercurrent of ambivalence in the founders about new members that caused the transmission of mixed messages to persons recruited for board service. This conflicting communication led to confusion over roles, responsibilities, and accountability for programmatic and artistic decisions. The value of the depth education experience to this organization was that it provided a constructive way of acknowledging the internal and sometimes unconscious barriers that were keeping the organization from attracting and developing a strong, diverse board membership.

An organization serving physically ill, disabled children asked for assistance in clarifying and managing the roles and responsibilities of board and staff and in developing cohesion and commitment around the organization's purpose and vision. The organization was several years old and had been started by a group of passionate health care givers from the sponsoring institution and spouses of employees of the same institution. The board was a hands-on board with dual functions of governance and administration. They managed to juggle both fairly well but were finding it increasingly stressful to combine them as the organization continued to serve more children and the challenge of financial survival increased.

One board member was looking at the possibility of affiliation with another organization, although the full board had not officially sanctioned this search. In fact, no one seemed to be very concerned about this. As the board went through the historical reflection and analysis of their existence in history, a pattern of a closed in-group within the board was revealed: 85 percent of the board's resignations had been of new members. It was the first time the group saw these resignations as a systemic rather than individual problem. Previous resignations had been viewed and experienced in individual and personal ways. This organization wanted to expand its membership and increase its leadership, so it was decided that it could not ignore this discovery. The board sought more information about its functioning and that of the organization that allowed it to see itself more truthfully. The focus shifted from why particular members left to why the organization was losing members and how it could retain them. The board was more motivated to examine its culture and to address its process for inviting and including new members. They questioned the inclusiveness of the mission, and when their retreat concluded, they had a plan to complete the planning process, rewrite their mission statement, review their organizational structure and board policies, and clarify their governance and administrative responsibilities. One change they immediately decided on was to institute the use of formal agendas at meetings and to have clearly defined purposes, tasks, and the action desired so that both new and experienced trustees knew what the focus of the meeting would be and what was expected of them. These practices have helped them develop a board of leaders who can focus on their trusteeship responsibilities.

It is a jolting experience of psychological dissonance when boards that perceive themselves as inclusive are observed to be engaging in practices and behaviors that reveal something quite different. In these instances, it is truly a matter of consciousness. The board's composition may change and become more diverse, but the patterns of communication and sharing of responsibility are still rooted in a past reality. For example, the inclusion of women members on a formerly all-male board is just the first of many steps in changing its practices and its composition. The board invested in developing the leadership of trustees will ask of itself and discuss more questions to prepare for such a change. What will it mean to have women on the board? Does involvement mean physical presence, verbal contributions, sharing of skill and expertise?

Such questions can lead to meaningful conversation about what it means to be inclusive and diverse and, if the dialogue is sustained long enough, to developing substantive inclusive practices.

Every board's conversation reflects the uniqueness of its identity and the particularity of its organizational culture; its responses to depth education will be influenced by these distinctions. The object of cultivating the practice of addressing the depth education questions is not to produce cookie-cutter trustees or to entrap boards in a formulaic approach to deciding issues of considerable complexity, but to improve their ability to make significant and positive contributions at the deepest and broadest levels of the organization's life—to be leaders, not just managers. This is the process of the development of trustee leaders who can hold the organization in trust. One example of the power that changing practices can have on the formation of trustee leaders is that of the board of a well-endowed private school that underwent an intensive evaluation in preparation for school certification. Its board members were nearly all from the same socioeconomic class, and many socialized together. Much information about the school was shared in these informal social settings, and board meetings tended to be rubber-stamp sessions. As the board tried to include a more racially and economically diverse membership, the process of its decision making became an increasing concern because of the exclusionary effect of the informal practices of decision making.

Diversification of boards always challenges the prevailing culture and necessitates a close examination of its assumptions, actions, practices, and motivation to change. The organization is confronted with change at levels unknown when a decision is made to be more inclusive. These are issues that would need to be addressed with the addition of any new board member, but if the members are from a social, professional, or economic strata notably different from that of the existing group, opportunities for information sharing, alliance building, and common understanding among board members may be seriously diminished. If there is not intentionality about including others in the informal, established communication network and keeping every board member informed, a marginalized subgroup can be created, and their contributions to the deliberative and decision-making processes lost.

Unless the organization's leadership recognizes that part of its membership has been inadvertently excluded or that its practices, however much a part of tradition, are now practices of classism and racism, then the integrity of the group is at stake.

In the aforementioned example, the board president realized that the responsibility of the board was going to entail much more than data gathering in the evaluation and accreditation process, and he implemented a depth education process that created opportunities for joint staff-board member discussions about the data they were collecting. Because this level of analysis originated from a mandate from an external authorizing body (the accreditation group), the board was able to open up a different path to making decisions and could begin to see the value of having all of its members better informed consistently. Once the accreditation process was finished, the board looked at ways it could continue to accumulate the kind of knowledge it had acquired. It began providing opportunities for longer discussion of topics and issues not in need of immediate action and that included all board members in the deliberation.

The board also started hosting informal budget orientation meetings for both new and seasoned board members in need of a review or introduction to more detailed information and explanation about the school's financial state. Board members could ask as many questions as they needed to at these meetings and were better prepared to reach good decisions at regular board meetings. Board members now have enough data to make informed decisions, and they converse about the philosophical and programmatic reasons underlying the numbers. This kind of depth preparation and complex reasoning in which trustees engage benefits the organization because it builds capacity. What could have been perceived as a threat to the organization's way of being—diversity of membership and evaluation—became opportunities for continual learning and development of its trustee leaders.

Depth education moves trustees into a larger contextual framework in which positional conflict can be discouraged. A trustee of a not-for-profit board in California was feeling exasperated by the factionalism that had resulted over a conflict in the group over the best way to fund a project for preadolescent girls. Hard lines had been drawn between those who favored an increase in membership dues and those who preferred using the principal from an endowment fund. As soon as the conflict became personal and positional, it became more difficult to engage in constructive dialogue. The board was advised to deescalate the conflict by withdrawing from a yes-no debate and returning to the history of the organization. During this process of discovery and examination, the board saw how the board and staff had responded in the past to comparable situations. The learning was then used to guide a discussion of what is currently in the best interests of the organization. The historical remembering enlarged the dialogue and opened up more options and choices for consideration. Helping current trustees remember examples of risk and recognize the factors involved in past successful or unsuccessful outcomes can sometimes help those who are entrenched in their positions to realize that they are part of a heritage that is worth keeping—or one that it may be time to discard.

Shared history can be common ground for a shared understanding that equips trustees to venture into unfamiliar territory, trusting in a larger tradition and wisdom. If individuals keep their positional hats on as they review history, they will screen out information that conflicts or creates discomfort. The exercise of trusteeship at such times is a matter of opening board members and staff to the possibility of change and of letting something new and unknown emerge. It is an experience of living in the neutral zone, an important state of transition that trustee leaders need to learn to lead through. In this state, a rush to decision may alleviate the board's immediate anxiety but do nothing to affect the real problem. The board may think that it has acted, but whether it exercised leadership is the more salient question. If it misses opportunities to address real problems, the problems may be driven underground, only to emerge in a more vigorous form later.

Not all processes of board behavior are as conscious as some of the examples in this chapter. Sometimes the behavior is unconscious and unavailable for observation, evaluation, or alteration. Any change in such a situation will most likely result from external expert analysis and intervention that can help the board see itself more truthfully.

A board that sees itself in a leadership role will examine the way it makes decisions and determine whether the processes it engages in are ones that do at least these four things:

- Take into consideration the organization's history
- Use mission as the standard for determining appropriate and ethical action
- Provide structure and space for developing trust, respect, and opportunities for ongoing learning
- Create space for the inclusion of all board members in discussion, problem formation, and solutions

The integration of depth education and the preparation of boards for leadership is ongoing work and enables a process of continual learning in which individual trustees and staff grow in their leadership capacities and abilities to transform organizations into cultures of leadership.

Chapter Fourteen

The Board as Leader

Governing bodies are the legally accountable holders of a community trust and are granted considerable authority over the institutions they serve. The delegation and exercise of their authority is an expression of a tradition of trusteeship and a legacy of leadership, for the authority invested in a board is affected not only by the law but also by historical and cultural forces and societal views of leadership.

We seem to have a profound ambivalence about leadership: we desire yet resist it, deify it yet distrust it. Our beliefs and views of leadership affect the ways we create, structure, and sustain organizations and communities. Our fundamental assumptions can shape a particular kind of leader and reinforce certain forms of leadership. If our belief is that leadership is an innate quality that only a select few possess, then leadership is the possession of an elite group, an activity engaged in by those who are "naturally gifted and talented," and the goal is to pick "the right person" for the position or task. The consequences of this perception can lead to a form of apartheid in leadership practice and education that can diminish individual initiative and ignore the capacities of many leaders in many arenas.

If we believe in the opposing view that everyone is a leader, then we might assume that leadership is solely a matter of desire and learned behavior and that anyone who wishes to be a leader can be taught to be one. This view reinforces the notion that leadership is primarily a matter of skill development and behavior modification, and shapes a definition of leadership that is visible and observable, concrete, action based, and measurable. There is a mammoth education and training culture based on this perception, and it perpetuates the equation that leadership equals doing. This perception reinforces a concretized, mechanistic view of leadership education that does not equip the learner with the capacity that is needed to solve complex, adaptive problems in a changing environment. While the intent of the belief that everyone is a leader is admirable in its inclusivity, the danger presented is an oversimplification of the outer skills and inner attributes needed for the development of authentic, capable leaders.

Competence is an external and internal capability with experience and substance to support it. An obsession with external competence can lead to focusing on visible skills and immediate outcomes rather than on inner work and development of the character. This perception of leadership can leave us transfixed on solutions before truly understanding what needs to be solved. If action equals leadership, then time for reflective, thoughtful reasoning and inner dialogue may be diminished.

An overemphasis on action and the equation of it with leadership can create an illusion of accomplishment when what is occurring is a form of wheel spinning. The normative tendency to do something immediately when confronted with a problem is strong. To do something feels better than the feared state of nothingness, even when the doing may be shortsighted or inappropriate. The leadership-as-action view is outcome oriented. The substance and complexity of issues can be missed or minimized. When a formulaic frenzy of activity is held up as leadership, we become enticed into a superficial understanding of what it means to lead, and our approach to problem solving becomes concrete and limited.

Dichotomous and limited views of leaders and leadership are philosophical and behavioral traps. We can engage in continuous debate about whether leadership is innate or learned, for the few or for the masses, whether it is doing or being, but it is becoming clearer that we need to cultivate and foster a different kind of leadership. As long as we think that the only valid way to develop leadership is through skill acquisition and serial activity untethered to inner values and an internal capacity for sound analytical and decision-making processes, the very things we need and seek—safe, healthy, effective individuals, organizations, and communities able to adapt constructively in times of great stress—will remain elusive.

Leadership and the education of leaders can become a mass-produced activity. The perception of few as leaders and all as leaders are the extremes on a continuum. Both are useful in certain circumstances, but when either is seen as the full definition of leadership, we lose the transformative nature of leadership.

The answers to what leader and leadership are reside between the extremes of aristocratic and pedestrian notions of leadership. Practitioners, researchers, and educators who seek a deeper meaning of leadership enter this expanse between the opposites—an area of paradox—with an appreciation for the deep terrain in which they have entered. It is foreign country to many, but only in this place is the opportunity to find some answers to the chronic problems of our time and of the future. It will be between the polarities where we can craft a reconciliation between the being and doing of leadership and mobilize people to clarify what matters most among competing needs and conflict values. It is in paradox where we can reach a fuller understanding of what leadership is and how we can better educate others for the responsibilities.

Financial scandals in not-for-profit organizations in the recent past have served as catalysts for a reexamination of what it means to lead and what needs to be done to educate individuals for governance. We have witnessed a damaging distrust of leadership in some organizations and, in a few cases, a questioning of the need for the continued existence of the organization itself. The executives of these organizations have been relieved of their positions; one was incarcerated. These organizations have suffered from damaged reputations and significant, if temporary, drops in public financial support. The loss of support in dollars has been significant; the loss of trust has been incalculable.

The public explanations of these crises came dangerously close to executive finger pointing. These individuals were portrayed as the primary perpetrators of the organization's misfortune in the organization's attempts to restore public trust and confidence. Nevertheless, none of these situations can escape the shared responsibility and accountability of those who govern these organizations. The development of capable governance leaders and the partnership between them and the executives will be required to restore trust.

The governing board of an organization is legally and ethically responsible for the organization's standards of conduct and its performance. The board is a special classification of volunteers called to serve the organization and represent the interests and needs of the broader community. When the public trust is betrayed, the broader community deserves an acknowledgment from the board for its responsibility. In the organizational crises already noted, there was no public acknowledgment through resignations or penalties levied on the boards. It is understandable that the public responses by the boards would seek to protect the organization and minimize any legal and financial liability, but it is equally imperative that boards in these kinds of situations perceive them as opportunities to evaluate themselves and the ways in which they have exercised their responsibilities of trusteeship. Postcrisis observation indicates that most of these boards immediately attended to issues of financial accountability and exercised greater scrutiny of day-to-day operations. In the heat of crises, responses like this seem reasonable and responsible; after all, if someone has misused funds, the first response should be to decrease or eliminate the opportunities for such an occurrence in the future. But if not much else is reviewed and changed, the deeper causes of the problems remain unexamined. Faced with the loss of public trust, the board needs to work to restore it. Its efforts need to include opportunities for the board to examine itself fully, question its governance and leadership performance, and establish practices and processes that will minimize the chances of malfeasance or the occurrence of other unethical behavior in the future.

When board leaders can develop a discipline of depth education and self-evaluation, they will decrease their culpability in future crises. To enable boards to respond differently means undergoing a seismic shift in their perceptions of what trusteeship is and what the responsibilities of governance leadership are. Most board members are committed, capable, and engaged persons, but if they fall into the trap of seeing their roles in primarily technical and positional terms, their ability to effect change at the deeper levels of organizational life will be seriously limited. A deeper awareness of the scope of their responsibilities as leaders could result in opportunities to discuss and integrate the concept of trusteeship. When crisis erupts and the board is caught unaware, its ignorance is more attributable to ignorance of the depth of the role of trustee leaders than to any deliberate, conscious negligence. Ignorance of matters that are central to the identity and survival of organizations places the organization at high risk, risk that can be greatly diminished when the depth practices of trusteeship are in place.

Having a busy, hard-working board means little unless what is keeping it busy are the core issues linked to the identity, performance, and survival of the organization. These core issues need to address the capacity and functioning of the board itself. What is the role of a board? What is the role of this particular board? What should the board know in order to carry out its role responsibly? For what is it responsible? To whom is it accountable? What does a board need to know to be trust holders of this organization? When does it need to know this information, and in what form? How can we become and continue to be a knowledgeable and deeply committed community of discernment and decision making? These are some of the important questions every governance group wrestles with if the members take their tenure seriously (and I think they do). In wrestling with them, boards can become truly engaged in the process of forming a body of trustees with an impressive capacity to lead.

Virtually every board knows it is responsible for hiring, evaluating, and firing the executive director, but few understand the responsibility they have for a parallel process: their own formation, evaluation, development, and termination. An annual evaluation and checkup, during which the current state of the board is ascertained and a determination of its prescription for health in the future can be done, would be valuable to the majority of not-for-profits. Self-assessment and planning for its own learning and development would focus the board on its special leadership role and its responsibility to be intentional in preparing for it.

The boards of many organizations are conflicted about, or resistant to, designating sufficient resources for their own education and development. This may be due to a residual belief in the notion of the innately gifted leader or from assuming that leadership comes with position. Much can be assumed about the leadership ability of trustees who occupy positions of authority and leadership in the community and have been successful in their professional endeavors. However, not many of the professional men and women sitting on governing bodies would allow a comparably composed group to determine the fate of their own companies or organizations without first investing in their training and ongoing education for such a responsibility. Most board members who lead an organization know how difficult it is to form a cohesive, competent team of diverse individuals to work productively, yet comparable thought does not seem to have been given to the need to put the same effort into the development of a leadership team comprising individuals from disparate institutions, cultural backgrounds, and perspectives so that they can exercise their governance responsibilities ethically and competently.

The not-for-profit sector needs help in overcoming a long history of providing minimal or insufficient education for those most responsible for the governance and leadership of organizations. Perhaps when there was a stronger sense of community and an explanation for voluntarism that connected deeply to a religious tradition, the desire to serve seemed sufficient. The loss of this second language and a sense of the common good so well described in *Habits of the Heart,* by Robert Bellah and his colleagues, means that assumptions about a shared value system or common vision can no longer prevail (Bellah, Sullivan, and Tipton, 1985).

Board ignorance and the loss of a second language and shared value system are a potentially lethal combination if they exist beyond the short term. Those who have served on or worked with such boards have firsthand knowledge about the enormous price paid when a wall of ignorance enshrouds a governing body and internal disconnections exist. The directors who work with such boards engage in what seems in the short term to be adaptive behavior in a crisis: protect the organization and the board. Certainly this is the natural response if anything threatens the existence of any organism. But what can happen is a continued segregation of the board from its real work and the critical issues of the organization. The crises within local and national organizations in the not-for-profit sector in the past decade may not translate into a national epidemic, and they in no way are harbingers of the demise of the not-for-profit sector, but we do need to watch and learn from them and allow them to be opportunities for us to address the troubling conditions in the professional and voluntary realms. These public betrayals of trust need public scrutiny and conversation, not for purposes of punishment but so we can learn about what went wrong and why.

In reality, boards operate more like a group of individual leaders than a leadership group. Although they are a collective that needs to work in partnership with executive directors and share authority and power, the most frequently used structures of management and governance are hierarchical and top-down. They have not engendered the kind of relationships, collaboration, and teamwork best able to govern organizations in the not-for-profit sector. Trustees who see leadership as an individual proposition rather than the management of a team of leaders in partnership with executive staff may be creating obstacles to achieving a stronger governance group. The perception of leadership in these ways works to restrict the commitment and creativity of staff, detracting the board from further development and from improving the skills and abilities necessary for leadership.

When the board perceives itself as a leader, and not only a management group, it is far better equipped to comprehend and carry out the larger tradition of philanthropy with the understanding that it is an integral part of the vast culture of giving and service. This identity places the board in a position to develop a wider and broader perspective from which to monitor the organization's efforts and to view and strategically plan the organization's response to the future. Without this deeper perspective and breadth of understanding, the board will find it difficult to overcome what is now a prevalent tendency to micromanage the day-to-day affairs of those primarily responsible for administration. When the board can assume this perspective, it places itself in a position of leadership. Staff can then trust the governance of the organization and can focus on being trustees of administration, programs, and clients.

Conclusion

The majority of organizations in the not-for-profit sector exist to serve a public and the public good. Their reason for existing establishes a special trust, one that obligates them to understand fully what it means to hold something in trust. Their shared existence links them together and gives powerful expression to the uniquely American legacy of caring for the common good. Their ability to acknowledge their covenantal origins, and to reclaim and live out this legacy, will have profound implications for the vitality of the not-for-profit sector and all who are touched by it.

The growth of the not-for-profit sector is exciting and challenging, and the increase of volunteers is a hopeful sign of both our compassion and our vision of ourselves as a democracy. Perhaps governance leaders have not strayed too far from the historical legacy of caring for the common good. The vast quantity of volunteers serving not-for-profit organizations is indicative of something positive. Perhaps it is a deeply rooted yearning to contribute in a meaningful way. Whatever the reasons, our attention and resources must turn to helping board volunteers to assume their unique responsibilities for leadership and service in the not-for-profit sector. Our expectations of those who volunteer, of those who govern, will shape how we educate and prepare them to fulfill their responsibilities. It is time for a different kind of education for trustees: education based on a depth understanding of the organization—its lived history, mission, publics, and future. This approach is foundational to the development of trusteeship and its effective expression. It is the basis of a trustee's capacity to lead from a depth understanding of what it really means to hold an organization in trust.

There are no absolute answers to how to have effective trustees, but we are striving to shift the focus of trustee education away from technical skills to include skill building and meaning making as essential elements. This shift is one of leadership development for not-for-profit boards.

We should be impatient with the litany of how busy board members are when it is used as an excuse for not providing the kind of leadership education and development needed in organizations and communities. We need to question whether time is really the issue. The problem is the lack of value we place on reflection and contemplation in our culture. Reflection somehow conjures up a state of passivity and inactivity that is antithetical to Western culture. Doing is being in our culture. Behavior that looks like nothing is going on or for which we can see no immediate result is devalued. We need different frameworks and metaphors for describing the value of depth education and reflection. Just as we cannot grow a plant from a seed in nine hours, neither can we transform a board in a weekend retreat. The seeds of trusteeship can be planted, and the conditions and care necessary for their growth can be provided and cultivated. We can make sure we have the best gardeners, but we still cannot speed up the pace of growth. Instant practices of education may have a place, but they are grossly insufficient. Periodically we need to take time out from our preoccupation with the concrete tasks in our lives and from obsession with time to examine and evaluate what we are doing, why we are doing it, for whom, and for what larger and longer term purpose.

The opportunities to develop a rich common life together in which we can create space where true community can be developed and practiced need to be maximized so that organizations and communities develop the capacities to address the important work waiting to be done. The not-for-profit sector is one of the few remaining places where a "company of strangers" (Palmer, 1990) is being transformed into some semblance of community. I know of no other place where there are more likely to be professionals and nonprofessionals, volunteers and staff, men and women, and individuals of varied economic and cultural backgrounds, all coming together to discuss issues that affect the quality of life in community. I know of few other places where dialogue about major social problems is encouraged and used in setting public policy.

Whatever the methodologies used to develop and prepare boards, they need to connect trustees to a much larger context of service, focused by the lens of the particular history and mission of the organization. This exploration of purpose and identity must be able to help the organization translate an enormous amount of information amassed about itself, its clients, and its community into significance, meaning, and service. The translation and meaning making must engender ethical and authentic responses. Whatever the approach used for board education, it is important to remember that the potential for responsible action is severely limited if the results do not include broadened perspective and deepened insight. Developing boards of leaders who can respond to reality responsibly means engaging them in a dynamic process of discovery, reflection, and analysis, infused with meaning and punctuated by action. This is the hardest work a board can engage in.

The belief that the actions of trustees and educators can influence and even transform society must grow and contribute to reshaping common approaches to board education and the pedagogy of leadership education. When it does, a new generation of governance leaders will have the capacity to hold individuals, organizations, and communities in trust.

Resource A: Organizational Assessment Form for Executive Staff

The following survey is to be completed by the organization's executive director and key staff members.

Date: _____

Name of Organization: _____

Address: _____

_____

Year founded: _____

1. What was the original mission of the organization?

2. What is the current mission of the organization?

3. What are the major differences between the original mission and the current mission? What do these differences reflect?

4. List clients served each year for five years. Categorize by year, type of clients, age, gender, race, and socioeconomic background.

5. Roster of staff (include job titles and years of employment):

6. Roster of trustees (include length of term, number of terms allowed, average length of time served by board members):

7. Annual budget: _____

8. Sources of funding and percentage of budget:

Sources	Amount of Funding	Percentage of Budget
Government	_____	_____
Membership fees	_____	_____
Individual contributions	_____	_____
Endowment fund	_____	_____
United Way	_____	_____
Foundations	_____	_____
Corporate	_____	_____
Other (specify)	_____	_____

9. Programs and expenditures by programs (list programs and their costs):

Program	Cost	Number Served
_____	_____	_____
_____	_____	_____
_____	_____	_____
_____	_____	_____
_____	_____	_____
_____	_____	_____

10. Characterize your financial status (cash flow, recent reductions, grants received, and so on). What, if any, major changes do you see ahead in your finances?

11. How does the organization plan for the future?

12. Other comments:

Resource B: Organizational Assessment Form for Governance Leaders

The following questions are asked of all board members via surveys or interviews or both.

Date: _____

Trustee's name: _____

Occupation: _____

Name of organization trustee is serving: _____

Length of time served on the board: _____

Board positions held and dates of service: _____

_____

_____

1. Describe your responsibilities as a trustee of [name of organization].

2. What is the organization's mission? How often is the mission reviewed and evaluated?

3. How do you see the mission reflected in your programs?

4. When did your organization last engage in planning?

5. Describe the planning process your organization has used in the past and what the results were.

6. What do you belicve the role of a trustee to be?

7. In order of importance, list the three most important responsibilities of trustees.

8. What is your evaluation of how effective the trustees in your organization are in carrying out these responsibilities?

9. Describe what enables trustees on your board to be effective and what impedes them from being effective.

10. How do your trustees evaluate your organization's effectiveness?

11. Who is primarily responsible for looking at the big picture in your organization? How is this responsibility carried out? How often?

12. Describe the preparation and education for serving on the board that the trustees of your organization receive. Be specific as to purpose, time, content, setting, length of time, and so on.

13. How would you characterize the trustees' relationship with the organization's executive director and staff?

14. When conflict arises between the board and director, how is it dealt with? Between board members?

15. How are trustees recognized when they have done an effective job?

16. How do trustees know that the executive director and staff are performing their duties and responsibilities well?

Resource C: Analysis and Summary of Executive and Governance Assessment

This summary form is completed by the trustee educator, using the answers from surveys, interviews, and review of other organizational data. This compilation and categorization of responses is used as a resource by the consultant working with the organization to write a comprehensive organizational assessment report. The bulleted items following each question indicate possible sources of the information.

Date: _____

Name of organization: _____

Address: _____

_____

1. What is the purpose of the organization? Is the purpose of the organization clearly defined?
   - Resource A, question 2
   - Resource B, questions 2 and 3
   - Interviews with trustees, staff, clients, and community representatives
   - Review of by-laws, organization documents, and other materials

2. How well is the organization's mission known and articulated?
   - Resource B, question 2
   - Mission statement and brochures
   - Interviews with staff, trustees, clients, and community representatives

3. How well is the mission understood by trustees, staff, clients, and community? What is done to accomplish this?
   - Resource B, questions 3 and 5
   - Interviews with a random sample of trustees, staff, clients, and community members

4. Does the organization have a vision for the future? Does it have a clearly stated process for defining the future direction?
   - Resource B, question 4
   - Interviews with president of board, executive director
   - Review of organization's documents and other materials

5. How do the organization's goals, objectives, and programs reflect its mission?
   - Resource B, questions 3, 4, and 5
   - Review of planning documents
   - Observation of programs

6. How do trustees define their primary responsibilities?
   - Resource B, questions 6 and 7
   - Interviews with the board president and several selected trustees and staff

7. Do the trustees include the role of leadership in their description of their responsibilities?
   - Resource B, questions 6 and 7

8. How effective is the board in carrying out its responsibilities?
   - Resource B, question 8
   - Observations of board meetings

9. How effective is the board in carrying out its leadership role?
   - Resource B, questions 8–11
   - Observations of board meetings

10. Who is seen as responsible for maintaining the big picture in the organization? How is this perspective maintained?
    - Resource B, questions 4 and 7–10
    - Interviews with executive director and president of board

11. What value do the trustees place on preparation and the on-going education of its board? (Give at least three examples to substantiate your answer.)
    • Resource B, questions 12 and 15
    • Interviews with executive director and president of board

12. How do the trustees describe their relationship to staff?
    • Resource B, questions 13 and 16
    • Interviews with and observations of staff and trustees

13. What processes exist for the trustees to evaluate agency and trustee effectiveness?
    • Resource B, questions 10, 15, and 16

14. How does the board manage differences and conflict?
    - Resource B, question 14
    - Observation of staff and board meetings

15. How are trustees recognized and rewarded for their effectiveness?
    - Resource B, question 15

16. Who are the organization's publics?
    - Resource A, questions 3 and 4
    - Interviews with trustees, staff, clients, and community representatives

17. How knowledgeable are the trustees about the publics the organization serves?
    • Interviews with trustees and staff

18. Assessment summary

19. Recommendations

Resource D:
Organizational Assessment for Selection for the PLANT™ Process

The board must meet the following criteria in order to be considered appropriate for PLANT training:

Yes _____   No _____   1. We are a not-for-profit organization.

Comments:

Yes _____   No _____   2. The board and staff have clarity about their roles and responsibilities and have an appropriate organizational structure to carry out their responsibilities.

Comments:

Yes _____ No _____   3. The organization's executive and governance leadership is in agreement about the organization's mission.

Comments:

Yes _____ No _____   4. The leadership of the organization is committed to excellence in service and programs.

Comments:

Yes _____ No _____   5. The organization's board is committed to allocating the resources required for preparation and participation in this board leadership development process.

Comments:

Yes _____   No _____   6. The board and executive staff understand and agree or are compatible
with the philosophy, beliefs, and values
that undergird the PLANT process.

Comments:

7. Additional comments:

Resource E:
Needs Assessment Survey
for Governance Leaders

Date: _____

Name: _____

Current position in the organization: _____

Length of time in current position: _____

Previous positions and dates of service to organization: _____

_____

_____

1. What issues or concerns do you believe need to have the attention of the board? Please be specific and explain why these need priority attention.

2. What will make this educational experience a successful one for you as an individual trustee? For the whole board?

3. What would make this a disappointing experience for you? For the board?

4. What are other critical issues facing the organization? How have these been dealt with in the past? In the present?

5. What are your specific hopes for this organization?

6. What are you prepared to do to make this educational experience for the board and executive staff a productive and useful one?

7. What three outcomes do you want to result from this experience?

Resource F:
Functions of the Resource
Committee

The resource committee provides a vital function in the preparation for trustee education and is one of the keys to a productive and useful experience. It needs to be representative of staff and trustees and, if appropriate, other volunteers. We recommend that those serving on the resource committee include key board members whose presence and efforts will reinforce the ownership of all trustees in this process. The committee should plan to begin this work four to six weeks before the depth education training. The consultants will serve as advisers to the resource committee as it prepares, providing an orientation session that outlines the purpose, responsibilities, tasks, and work schedule. The resource committee will take responsibility for the following:

- Initial preparation of the history time line
- Conducting or assigning trustees to interviews for "Learning from Our Publics" (see Resource H)
- Assisting in making arrangements for the physical space, dates, and times for the depth education training and other resources required for the training

Resource G:
Sample Philanthropic
Time Line

This time line was developed by Susan Wisely and Linda Engle and executed by Lynn Flanagan.

Senate
Subcommittee for
Family and Human
Services

House Select Committee
on Children, Youth
and Families

Challenger
space shuttle's
maiden voyage

Congress
approves $37
billion tax cut

Job Training
Partnership Act—
federal grants for
job training

Adoption
Assistance and
Child Welfare Act

IBM introduces
personal computer

First implant of
permanent artificial
heart in human

Reagan wins
presidency

Halley's Comet
returns after 77 years

Terrorists kill 241
marines in suicide
bombing in Beirut

Recession ends
but inflation
continues

Prince Charles weds
Lady Diana Spencer

New York Fire
Department hires
women

Mount St. Helens
erupts

U.S. interest rates
around 16%

Sally Ride becomes
first American
woman in space

Senate votes to eliminate
busing for purposes of
racial integration

Unemployment
soars

President
Anwar Sadat
of Egypt
assassinated

Equal Rights
Amendment fails
ratification

U.S. troops land
on Grenada

| 1980 | 1981 | 1982 | 1983 | 1984 |

INDEPENDENT
SECTOR

Sandra Day
O'Connor—
first woman on
Supreme Court

Cherokee Nation
Youth Leadership
Program

Edna McConnell
Clark Foundation—
Family Preservation
Program

Total giving for
philanthropy is
$48.74 billion

National Crime
Prevention Council

Safe Sitter

First report of AIDS
or HIV virus in U.S.

Students Against
Driving Drunk
(SADD)

22,088 grantmaking
foundations in U.S.

Miriam and Peter
Haas Fund

W. T. Grant Foundation
Faculty Scholars Program
in mental health
of children

Walter Annenberg gives
$150 million to fund joint
Annenberg/Corporation
for Public Broadcasting
project

National Commission
on Excellence
in Education,
A Nation at Risk

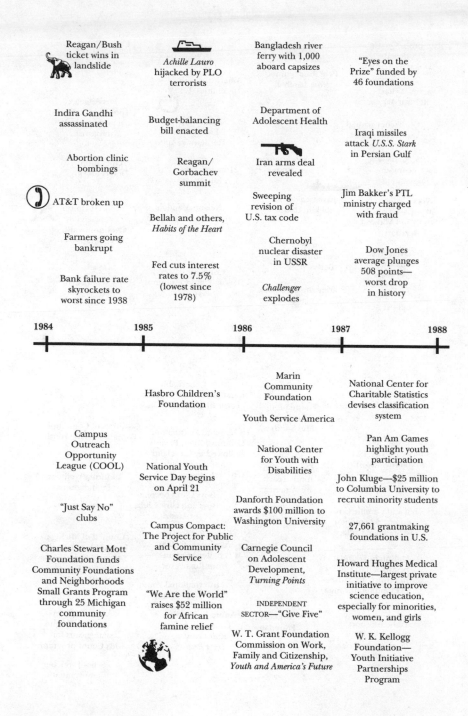

Reagan/Bush
ticket wins in
landslide

Achille Lauro
hijacked by PLO
terrorists

Bangladesh river
ferry with 1,000
aboard capsizes

"Eyes on the
Prize" funded by
46 foundations

Indira Gandhi
assassinated

Budget-balancing
bill enacted

Department of
Adolescent Health

Iraqi missiles
attack *U.S.S. Stark*
in Persian Gulf

Abortion clinic
bombings

Reagan/
Gorbachev
summit

Iran arms deal
revealed

AT&T broken up

Bellah and others,
Habits of the Heart

Sweeping
revision of
U.S. tax code

Jim Bakker's PTL
ministry charged
with fraud

Farmers going
bankrupt

Chernobyl
nuclear disaster
in USSR

Dow Jones
average plunges
508 points—
worst drop
in history

Bank failure rate
skyrockets to
worst since 1938

Fed cuts interest
rates to 7.5%
(lowest since
1978)

Challenger
explodes

1984   1985   1986   1987   1988

Hasbro Children's
Foundation

Marin
Community
Foundation

National Center for
Charitable Statistics
devises classification
system

Youth Service America

Campus
Outreach
Opportunity
League (COOL)

National Youth
Service Day begins
on April 21

National Center
for Youth with
Disabilities

Pan Am Games
highlight youth
participation

John Kluge—$25 million
to Columbia University to
recruit minority students

"Just Say No"
clubs

Danforth Foundation
awards $100 million to
Washington University

Campus Compact:
The Project for Public
and Community
Service

27,661 grantmaking
foundations in U.S.

Charles Stewart Mott
Foundation funds
Community Foundations
and Neighborhoods
Small Grants Program
through 25 Michigan
community
foundations

Carnegie Council
on Adolescent
Development,
Turning Points

Howard Hughes Medical
Institute—largest private
initiative to improve
science education,
especially for minorities,
women, and girls

"We Are the World"
raises $52 million
for African
famine relief

INDEPENDENT
SECTOR—"Give Five"

W. T. Grant Foundation
Commission on Work,
Family and Citizenship,
Youth and America's Future

W. K. Kellogg
Foundation—
Youth Initiative
Partnerships
Program

Bush/Quayle
defeat
Dukakis/Bentsen

Pete Rose banned
from baseball

Clean Air Act

Family Welfare
Reform Act

Americans with
Disabilities Act

Los Angeles
police brutalize
unarmed black
motorist

Gorbachev named
Soviet president

East and West
Germany reunite

U.S./Canada
free-trade
agreement

San Francisco
earthquake

Iraq invades
Kuwait

Operation
Desert Storm

Worst drought in
50 years—farms in
South and Midwest
devastated

Exxon Valdez oil
spill in Alaska

Nelson Mandela
released from prison
after 27 years

Soviet Union
replaced by
Commonwealth of
Independent States

Iran-Iraq War
ends after
eight years

Protesters
dismantle the
Berlin Wall

Family
Support Act

Tiananmen Square
massacre

Congress passes
National and Community
Service Act

Persian Gulf
War

1988	1989	1990	1991	1992

Indiana Youth
Institute

31,996 charitable
foundations in U.S., with
assets of $137.6 billion

Foundation
for the
Mid South

Cleveland Foundation
Commission on Poverty
followed by Cleveland
Community Building
Initiative

Coalition of Community
Foundations for Youth

38,042,000
Americans (20.4%)
do volunteer work

Mobile
Corporation
funds Teach
for America

California Wellness
Foundation

Boys Clubs become
Boys and Girls Clubs
of America

Bill and Camille Cosby
donate $20 million
to Spelman College

Teach for America
receives $500,000
challenge grant
from Ross Perot

Council of Michigan
Foundations launches
$47 million Michigan
Community Foundation
Youth Project

McKnight Foundation
begins Aid to Families
in Poverty Initiative—
$13 million through
1993

International Youth
Foundation

Lisbeth Schorr,
*Within Our Reach:
Breaking the Cycle
of Disadvantage*

Annenberg
Foundation

Annie E. Casey
Foundation,
*Kids Count
Data Book*

Annie E. Casey
Foundation begins
state grants for
Kids Count program

School voucher
movement

Family Preservation and
Support Services Act
passed by Congress

Canada, Mexico, and U.S.
sign North American
Free Trade Agreement

"Contract with
America"

Corporation for National
Service created to
administer AmeriCorps,
National Senior Service
Corps, and Learn and
Serve America

Clinton/Gore
win election

Personal
Responsibility and
Work Opportunity
Reconciliation Act

Ken Starr
appointed
independent
prosecutor

14.2% of U.S.
population living
below poverty line

World Trade
Center bombed

75th anniversary
of women's suffrage

Los Angeles riots

Civil War
in Rwanda

| 1992 | 1993 | 1994 | 1995 | 1996 |

Samuel Walton
dies at 74

Walter Annenberg gives
$500 million to nation's
public schools, bringing
his total gifts to
education for 1993
to nearly $1 billion

Foundation
for New Era
Philanthropy files
for bankruptcy

William Aramony—
United Way scandal

Istook proposes
amendment to limit
lobbying by groups that
receive federal grants

Robert Wood
Johnson Foundation
supports state
initiative to
strengthen families

Vice President Quayle
criticizes "Murphy Brown"

40,140 grantmaking
foundations in U.S.

26% of children living
in single-parent families

National Commission on
Teaching and America's
Future funded by
Rockefeller and Carnegie
Foundations

Family Support
Initiative at Boys
and Girls Clubs
supported by Annie E.
Casey Foundation

Oprah Winfrey—$1 million
to Spelman College

Fidelity Investments
Charitable Gift Fund

Magic Johnson—$5 million
to West Los Angeles Church
of God and Christ

Indiana Youth Institute—
"High Hopes, Long Odds"

National Youth Employment
Coalitions—Promising and
Effective Practice Network
(PEPNet)

Children's Health Insurance Program—$4 billion/year to cover uninsured children

Adoption and Safe Families Act

Balanced Budget Act— welfare reform bill

President's Summit for America's Future— "America's Promise, The Alliance for Youth"

Taxpayer Relief Act— $400 child tax credit, $1,500 education incentive

Mother Teresa, Nobel Peace Prize winner, dies

Ken Starr forwards report to Congress

Princess Diana, known for charity the world over, killed in car crash

Charitable choice legislation

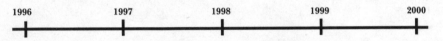

| 1996 | 1997 | 1998 | 1999 | 2000 |

Charitable giving in U.S. is $150.7 billion

Ted Turner gives $1 billion to United Nations causes, with emphasis on women, children, and environment

Council on Foundations celebrates 50th anniversary

Kathryn Albertson— $660 million to support public education in Idaho

Robert Wood Johnson Foundation begins posting summary reports of completed grants on Internet

George Soros— $500 million to projects in Russia

American Assembly report on American philanthropy

First baby boomers turn 50

Bill Gates—$200 million to Gates Library Foundation, $10 million to Lakeside School

Annie E. Casey Foundation plans five-year initiative on neighborhood transformation and family strengthening

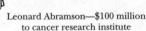

Leonard Abramson—$100 million to cancer research institute

Casey "Starting Early, Starting Smart" project in 12 communities

American Youth Policy Forum—*Some Things DO Make a Difference for Youth*—evaluation of 49 youth interventions

Casey Outcomes and Decision-Making Project explores managed care approach to child welfare

Youth and Philanthropy projects in Michigan and Indiana funded by Kellogg and Lilly Foundations

Heinz Endowment begins Early Childhood Initiative in Pittsburgh's poorest areas

Resource H: Learning from Our Publics Surveys

Learning from Our Publics
Community Leader Survey

Arrange appointments with community leaders who are not members of your board. Your primary purpose for the interview is to listen to *their* insights and understanding.

Explain that the purpose of conducting these interviews is for your organization to learn more about itself, its publics, and the organization's relationship to the larger community.

1. What do you know about this organization? (Use your organization's name.)
2. What is your understanding of this organization's mission?
3. Why do you think this organization needs to exist?
4. What contributions do you see this organization making to the larger community?
5. How effective is this organization?
6. What does it do well?
7. What doesn't it do well? How can it improve?
8. What do you think will be the major issues confronting our community in the next five to ten years?
9. What major national, state, or local trends do you see that we should be concerned about?
10. How might our organization be responsive to these issues?

Learning from Our Publics
Client Survey

Make arrangements to conduct several client interviews. (Staff can assist with scheduling these interviews.) Client interviews should be done only with the permission of the client, and confidentiality needs to be assured. Arrange to have a setting for the interviews that ensures comfort and privacy.

1. How did you hear about this organization? (Use your organization's name.)
2. Why did you choose to come to this organization?
3. Why is this organization needed?
4. What do you think this organization believes in?
5. What services does the organization provide?
6. Who can receive assistance from this organization?
7. How would you evaluate the organization's programs?
8. What would you like to see offered here that is not being offered now?
9. How could the organization improve?
10. What concerns or issues do you think this organization needs to address in the future?

Learning from Our Publics
Public-at-Large Survey

Strike up some impromptu conversations with individuals on the street, in church, in your office elevator, at gas stations, playgrounds, and so on. Have as many of these "chance" conversations as you can. Or your organization may want to set up a booth in several public gathering places and conduct random interviews with people; this approach might be more comfortable for both interviewer and interviewee.

Explain that your organization is gathering information to evaluate itself so that it can better serve the community.

1. What do you know about this organization? (Use your organization's name.)
2. What is the mission of this organization?
3. Who are the people we serve?
4. What programs and services do we offer?
5. If you needed our services, what would make you choose to come to us?
6. What contribution does this organization make to the larger community?
7. What do we do well?
8. How can we improve?
9. What do you think are the major problems we'll need to face in the next five to ten years?
10. What major national, state, or local trends do you see that we should be concerned about?

References

Bellah, R., Sullivan, W. M., and Tipton, S. M. *Habits of the Heart: Individualism and Commitment in American Life.* Berkeley: University of California Press, 1985.

Bennis, W., and Nanus, B. *Leaders: The Strategies for Taking Charge.* New York: HarperCollins, 1985.

Bridges, W. *Transitions: Making Sense of Life's Changes.* Reading, Mass.: Addison-Wesley, 1980.

Campbell, J. *The Hero with a Thousand Faces.* (2nd ed.) Princeton, N.J.: Princeton University Press, 1969. (Originally published 1949.)

Carnegie, A. "The Gospel of Wealth." In B. O'Connell (ed.), *America's Voluntary Spirit: A Book of Readings.* New York: Foundation Center, 1983.

Dudley, C. "History as a Source of Identity." *Trustee Educator,* 1990, *1*(1).

Dykstra, C. "Vision and Leadership." *Initiatives in Religion,* 1994, *3*(1).

Ellis, S., and Noyes, K. *By the People: A History of Americans as Volunteers.* (Rev. ed.) San Francisco: Jossey-Bass, 1990.

Greenleaf, R. *Servant Leadership: A Journey into the Nature of Legitimate Power and Greatness.* Ramsey, N.Y.: Paulist Press, 1977.

Greenleaf, R. *On Becoming a Servant-Leader.* (D. M. Frick, L. C. Spears, eds.) San Francisco: Jossey-Bass, 1996.

Hall, P. D. *Inventing the Nonprofit Sector and Other Essays on Philanthropy, Voluntarism, and Nonprofit Organizations.* Baltimore: John Hopkins University Press, 1992.

Heifetz, R. *Leadership Without Easy Answers.* Cambridge, Mass.: Belknap Press, 1994.

Hodgkinson, V. A., Weitzman, M. N., Toppe, C. M., and Noga, S. M. *Nonprofit Almanac, 1992–1993: Dimensions of the Independent Sector.* San Francisco: Jossey-Bass, 1992.

Hyde, L. *The Gift Imagination and the Erotic Life of Property.* New York: Vintage Books, 1983.

INDEPENDENT SECTOR. *Giving and Volunteering in the United States.* Washington, D.C.: INDEPENDENT SECTOR, 1996.

Lynn, R. W. "Penetrating the Mystery of Leadership Through Depth Education." In Lilly Endowment, *Annual Report.* Indianapolis, Ind.: Lilly Endowment, 1984.

O'Neill, M. *The Third America: The Emergency of the Nonprofit Sector in the United States.* San Francisco: Jossey-Bass, 1989.

Palmer, P. *The Company of Strangers: Christians and the Renewal of America's Public Life.* New York: Crossroad, 1990.

Parks Daloz, L., Keen, C. H., Keen, J. P., and Daloz Parks, S. *Common Fire: Lives of Commitment in a Complex World.* Boston: Beacon Press, 1996.

Prelinger, C. *Episcopal Women: Gender, Spirituality and Commitment in an American Mainline Denomination.* New York: Oxford University Press, 1992.

Rockefeller, J. "The Third Sector." In B. O'Connell (ed.), *America's Voluntary Spirit: A Book of Readings.* New York: Foundation Center, 1983.

Schein, E. *Organizational Culture and Leadership.* San Francisco: Jossey-Bass, 1990.

Schwartz, B. *The Battle for Human Nature: Science, Morality, and Modern Life.* New York: Norton, 1986.

Tocqueville, A. de. *Democracy in America.* (J. P. Mayer, ed.) New York: Doubleday, 1969. (Originally published 1830.)

Winthrop, J. "A Model of Christian Charity." In E. Morgan (ed.), *Puritan Political Ideas, 1558–1794.* New York: Bobbs-Merrill, 1965.

Wisely, D. S. *A Foundation's Relationship to Its Publics: Legacies and Lessons for the Lilly Endowment.* (Essay.) Indianapolis: Indiana University Center on Philanthropy, 1998.

Further Reading

Bettelheim, B. *The Uses of Enchantment: The Meaning and Importance of Fairy Tales.* New York: Knopf, 1976.

Conger, J. *Spirit at Work: Discovering the Spirituality in Leadership.* San Francisco: Jossey-Bass, 1994.

Donovan, M. S. *A Different Call: Women's Ministries in the Episcopal Church, 1850–1920.* Wilton, Conn.: Morehouse-Barlow, 1986.

Kimelman, R. *Tsedakah and Us.* New York: National Jewish Resource Center, 1982.

Palmer, P. *An Organization Is Like a Tree: A Resource for Trustee Educators.* Indianapolis, Ind.: Trustee Leadership Development, 1991.

Titmuss, R. *The Gift Relationship: From Human Blood to Social Policy.* New York: Pantheon Books, 1971.

Tyler Scott, K. *Cultivating Trusteeship: The Care and Tending of the Nonprofit Board.* Indianapolis, Ind.: Trustee Leadership Development, 1995.

Tyler Scott, K., Hoover, A., Wakefield, J., Turner, P., and Wisely, S. *Individual and Community Trusteeship Manual.* Indianapolis, Ind.: Trustee Leadership Development, 1991.

Tyler Scott, K., Hoover, A., Wakefield, J., Turner, P., and Wisely, S. *Trustee Leadership Development Board Leadership Development Manual.* Indianapolis, Ind.: Trustee Leadership Development, 1997.

Weisbrod, B. *The Nonprofit Economy.* Cambridge, Mass.: Harvard University Press, 1988.

Index